# The Grammar Handbook 1

A handbook for teaching Grammar and Spelling

## Sara Wernham and Sue Lloyd
### Illustrated by Lib Stephen

Edited by Rachel Stadlen

Jolly Learning

UK Edition first published March 2000
This US and Canada Edition published December 2000

Jolly Learning Ltd
Tailours House
High Road
Chigwell
Essex
IG7 6DL
United Kingdom

Tel: 011 44 20 8501 0405
Fax: 011 44 20 8500 1696

www.jollylearning.com

© Sara Wernham and Sue Lloyd, 2000 (text)
© Lib Stephen and Sara Wernham, 2000 (illustrations)

Printed and bound in England.

All blackline masters may be freely copied by teachers, without permission, if the number of copies is not more than is needed in their school or college. For other copies (such as for an external resource center), written permission must be obtained.

The blackline masters in this book use "Sassoon Infant," a typeface designed for children learning to read and write. Sassoon is a registered trademark of Sassoon and Williams. For more information see the following website: www.clubtype.co.uk

*The front cover shows two children doing the action for verbs in the past tense.*

*The page numbers in this book have been kept within the binding at the base of each page, so that the numbers do not appear on copies of the reproducible pages.*

ISBN 1 870946 86 3

# Acknowledgements

Our sincere thanks go first to Professor Alice Coleman, whose work has been an inspiration to us and a profound influence on this project. We are likewise indebted to Jennifer Chew O.B.E., for her invaluable expertise.

We are grateful also to Trudy Wainwright and the staff of St Michael's Primary School, Stoke Gifford, as of course to our colleagues at Woods Loke Primary School. Their hard work and support in testing our material has greatly benefited this book.

Finally we would like to thank Terry and Patty Clark of Palatine, Illinois, for all their help in preparing this edition for the US and Canada.

# Contents

## PART 1

Introduction   1
Teaching Ideas for Grammar   3
Teaching Ideas for Spelling   14

## PART 2   Reproducible Material

Reproducible Section 1 – Grammar and Spelling Lesson Sheets   21

| Week | Spelling | Grammar | |
|---|---|---|---|
| 1 | ‹sh› | Rainbow capitals | 26 |
| 2 | ‹ch› | Sentence pasting | 30 |
| 3 | ‹th› | Sentences | 34 |
| 4 | ‹ng› | Capital letters | 38 |
| 5 | ‹qu› | Proper nouns | 42 |
| 6 | ‹or› | Common nouns | 46 |
| 7 | Short vowels | Alphabetical order | 50 |
| 8 | Short vowels | "a" or "an" | 54 |
| 9 | ‹ff› | Plurals | 58 |
| 10 | ‹ll› | Pronouns | 62 |
| 11 | ‹ss› / ‹zz› | Initial blends wheel | 66 |
| 12 | ‹ck› | Initial blends | 70 |
| 13 | Vowels | Alphabetical order | 74 |
| 14 | ‹a_e› | Verbs | 78 |
| 15 | ‹i_e› | Conjugating verbs | 82 |
| 16 | ‹o_e› | Past tense | 86 |
| 17 | ‹u_e› | Doubling rule | 90 |
| 18 | ‹wh› | Future | 94 |

| Week | Spelling | Grammar | |
|------|----------|---------|------|
| 19 | ‹ay› | Alphabetical order | 98 |
| 20 | ‹ea› | Nouns | 102 |
| 21 | ‹igh› | Adjectives | 106 |
| 22 | ‹y› | Adjectives | 110 |
| 23 | ‹ow› | Final blends | 114 |
| 24 | ‹ew› | Compound words | 118 |
| | | | |
| 25 | ‹ou› | Alphabetical order | 122 |
| 26 | ‹ow› | Verbs | 126 |
| 27 | ‹oi› | Adverbs | 130 |
| 28 | ‹oy› | Adverbs | 134 |
| 29 | ‹ar› | ‹es› Plurals | 138 |
| 30 | ‹al› | Antonyms | 142 |
| | | | |
| 31 | ‹nk› | Alphabetical order | 146 |
| 32 | ‹er› | Speech marks | 150 |
| 33 | ‹ir› | Word web | 154 |
| 34 | ‹ur› | Questions | 158 |
| 35 | ‹au› | Questions | 162 |
| 36 | ‹aw› | Review | 166 |

| | | |
|---|---|---|
| Reproducible Section 2 – | Master Sheets | 170 |
| Reproducible Section 3 – | Flash Card Sheets | 174 |
| Reproducible Section 4 – | Spelling and Tricky Word Sheets | 186 |

## Extra Activities

| | | |
|---|---|---|
| Reproducible Section 5 – | Alphabet Sheets | 201 |
| Reproducible Section 6 – | "Sentence Pasting" Sheets | 205 |
| Reproducible Section 7 – | "Pull-Out Plurals" Sheet | 209 |
| Reproducible Section 8 – | "Verb Bees" Sheet | 211 |
| Reproducible Section 9 – | "Adjective Snake" Sheets | 213 |
| Reproducible Section 10 – | "Compound Birds" Sheet | 217 |

# Introduction

*The Grammar Handbook 1* is designed to follow *The Phonics Handbook*. It is intended to:

- introduce some basic elements of grammar,
- teach spelling systematically,
- improve vocabulary and comprehension,
- reinforce the teaching in *The Phonics Handbook*, and
- extend the students' phonic knowledge.

The teaching is multisensory, active and progresses at a challenging pace. It is especially suitable for young children. Each part of speech, for example, is taught with its own action and color. The actions enliven the teaching, and make the learning easier. The colors, which are useful for identifying parts of speech in sentences, match those used by Montessori Schools. Like *The Phonics Handbook*, *The Grammar Handbook 1* provides all the essential teaching ideas, and can be used alone. However, if possible, use it with the companion *Jolly Grammar Big Book 1*, to help in teaching each new concept. The *Jolly Phonics Cards* and *Inky Mouse puppet* will also be very useful.

## Students' achievement

The most dramatic improvements from using *Jolly Grammar* will be in the students' writing. The students will spell and punctuate more accurately, use a wider vocabulary, and have a clearer understanding of how language works.

In their first year at school, *Jolly Phonics* teaches students to write independently, by listening for the sounds in words and choosing letters to represent the sounds. This enables the students to write pages of news and stories. It is a joy to read their work and to see the great pride and confidence they derive from their newly-acquired skill. However, it is important to build on this foundation in the following year. *Jolly Grammar* provides teaching ideas for developing writing skills. The students become more aware that they are writing for a purpose: that their words are intended to be read and understood. They learn that writing is easier to understand if it is grammatically correct, accurately spelled, well-punctuated and neatly written – and that if the words used are interesting too, their writing can give real pleasure. Even in the early stages, it is valuable for students to have a simple understanding of this long-term goal.

# The format of *The Grammar Handbook 1*

The program consists primarily of reproducible activity sheets for two lessons a week. Each lesson is designed to be about one hour in duration, and material is provided for 36 weeks. Teaching ideas are offered alongside each activity sheet.

There are two elements to the program, namely spelling and grammar. Each week the first lesson is devoted to spelling and the second to grammar. These terms are loosely used and there is some overlapping: punctuation, vocabulary development and alphabet work are among the areas covered in both spelling and grammar lessons. This is deliberate: when mixed together, the two elements complement each other.

The teaching is intended to be envisaged as part of a broader literacy program. If two days' literacy sessions are devoted to *Jolly Grammar* each week, this leaves three for other areas, such as comprehension, group reading, independent and creative writing, and handwriting practice. The students should be shown how spelling and grammar relate to their other work, such as comprehension exercises, reading and independent writing. For instance, if they have recently covered compound words, and there is an example of one in the poem they are studying, the students should be encouraged to look for it.

The teaching ideas on the page opposite each activity sheet give useful suggestions and reminders. More detailed explanations and advice are provided in the following two chapters: "Teaching Ideas for Grammar" and "Teaching Ideas for Spelling."

To avoid confusion, *Jolly Grammar* follows the convention of using different symbols to distinguish between letter names and letter sounds. Letter names are indicated by the symbols ‹ ›, e.g. "Ship" begins with the letter ‹s›. By contrast, letter sounds are indicated by the symbols / / , e.g. "Ship" begins with the /sh/ sound.

# Teaching ideas for grammar

The benefits of learning grammar are cumulative. To begin with, a knowledge of grammar will give the students more conscious control over the clarity and quality of their writing. Later it will also help them to understand more complicated texts, learn foreign languages with greater ease, and use Standard English in their speech.

Spoken language is living and varies from region to region. The grammar we first learn, through our speech, varies accordingly. However, sometimes there is a need for uniformity. This uniformity improves communications, and is one of the main ways of uniting people in the English-speaking world. An awareness of this helps students who do not speak Standard English to understand that the way they speak is not wrong, but that it has not been chosen as the standard for the whole country. The students need to learn the standard form of English, as well as appreciating their own vernacular.

In their first year of *Jolly Grammar*, the students begin to develop an understanding of how their language works, and are taught some of the accepted grammatical conventions. The teaching aims to give an elementary understanding that we speak and write in sentences, and that the words we use fall into categories. The categories are known as parts of speech. Those introduced in *The Grammar Handbook 1* are nouns, pronouns, verbs, adjectives and adverbs. The students learn to use verbs to indicate whether something is happening in the past, present or future.

The term "grammar" is used broadly with students of this age. Definitions of the parts of speech, and of what constitutes a sentence, have necessarily been simplified to age-appropriate "working definitions." As the students grow older, the definitions can be expanded and refined.

With all teaching there must be a degree of repetition. This is particularly so when teaching a new discipline like grammar. Every lesson should include some review. Suggestions for review are provided in the teacher's notes opposite the activity sheets. However, teachers should feel free to use their own judgment as to which areas their students need to review.

## Proper Nouns

A noun denotes a person, place or thing. There are four kinds: common nouns (e.g. "bed"), proper nouns (e.g. "Matthew"), abstract nouns (e.g. "kindness") and collective nouns (e.g. "the team"). *The Grammar Handbook 1* begins by introducing proper nouns, since the students are already indirectly familiar with them through their own names. Children like to work with their names, and already know that they start with a capital letter.

A proper noun is the particular name given to a:

- person, including that person's last name and title;
- place: e.g. river, mountain, park, street, town, state or province, country;
- building: e.g. school, house, library, swimming pool, theater; and
- date: e.g. day of the week, month, holiday.

Proper nouns start with a capital letter. When we refer to people, places, days, etc. by their proper names, we use capital letters: for example, we use capital letters for "Anna," "Mount Everest" and "Monday," but not for "girl," "mountain" or "tomorrow." The capital letters indicate that the name is important. Children can understand that they are themselves important, since they are unique, and that this is why their own names start with a capital letter.

Action: The action for a proper noun is to touch one's forehead with the index and middle fingers. These are the fingers used for "name" in American Sign Language.

Color: The color for nouns is black.

## Common Nouns

Only concrete nouns are taught in *The Grammar Handbook 1*. Abstract nouns (e.g. "happiness") are more difficult for young students to grasp.

Everything we can see has a name by which we can refer to it. The students enjoy looking in the classroom for examples of objects, such as "table," "chair," "light," "carpet," "ruler," "pencil." As these names are not specific to any one object, but refer to tables, chairs, etc. in general, they are called common nouns and not proper nouns. At this stage the students find it useful to think of nouns as the names for things they can see and touch. To help the students decide if a word is a noun, they can see whether it makes sense to say the word "a," "an" or "the" before it, e.g. "the table," "a chair," "an elephant." ("A," "an" and "the" are the three articles, which are explained later.)

Action: The action for a common noun is to touch one's forehead with all the fingers of one hand.

Color: The color for nouns is black.

In general children understand the concept of nouns easily, and have no trouble when asked to think of examples. Identifying nouns in sentences is more difficult, but comes with practice. In any spare moments, encourage the students to identify the nouns in sentences on the board, or in big books.

# Plurals

Most nouns change in the plural, i.e. when they describe more than one. *The Grammar Handbook 1* introduces two regular ways the plural can be formed. The first is by adding an ‹s› to the noun, as in "dogs," "cats," "girls" and "boys." The second applies to those nouns which end with ‹sh›, ‹ch›, ‹s›, ‹z› or ‹x›. These words usually form the plural by adding ‹es›, as in "wishes," "lunches," "kisses" and "foxes." When children listen carefully they can hear the different sounds produced by the ‹s› and ‹es› endings. The plural endings ‹s› and ‹es› often sound like /z/ and /iz/, as in "dogs" and "boxes." Knowing that these words are plurals will help the students remember to spell the /z/ sound with an ‹s›.

Irregular, or tricky, plurals (e.g. "children"), are not introduced in *The Grammar Handbook 1*.

# Personal Pronouns

Pronouns are the little words used to replace nouns. *The Grammar Handbook 1* introduces the personal pronouns only. The relative pronouns (e.g. "who"), possessive pronouns (e.g. "mine" and "my") and reflexive pronouns (e.g. "myself") can be taught when the students are older.

Without pronouns, language would become boring and repetitive. To illustrate this, give the students an example of a story without pronouns, e.g. "Jenny, Eric and Hannah decided to go to the zoo. Jenny, Eric and Hannah prepared the food and then Jenny, Eric and Hannah set off." With the pronoun "they," this kind of repetition can be avoided. Examples of this sort help the students to understand the function of pronouns. They can appreciate why the word "pronoun" has the word "noun" in it, once they recognize that pronouns replace nouns.

There are eight personal pronouns:

|  |  |
|---|---|
| I | (first person singular) |
| you | (second person singular) |
| he | (third person singular) |
| she | (third person singular) |
| it | (third person singular) |
| we | (first person plural) |
| you | (second person plural) |
| they | (third person plural) |

Although in modern English the second person pronoun "you" is used for both singular and plural, this is not the case in many foreign languages. In order to make learning such languages easier later on, *Jolly Grammar* introduces students to the distinction between "you" used in the singular and "you" used in the plural.

| Actions: | I | – | point to self |
|---|---|---|---|
| | you | – | point to someone else |
| | he | – | point to a boy |
| | she | – | point to a girl |
| | it | – | point to the floor |
| | we | – | point in a circle to include self and others |
| | you | – | point to two other people |
| | they | – | point to the next-door class |

Color: The color for pronouns is pink.

# Verbs

A verb denotes what a person or a thing does, and can describe an action, an event, a state or a change. It is easiest for students to think of verbs as "doing words" at first. Ask each student for an example of something they do, with the word "to" before it, so that they give verbs in the infinitive form, e.g. "to run," "to hop," "to sing," "to play." This is not something they find difficult.

Since verbs in English are very complicated, *The Grammar Handbook 1* introduces only the simple tenses. For the verb root "cook," for instance, the infinitive is "to cook," the simple present tense is "cook," the simple past tense is "cooked," and the simple future is "will cook." Later, when the students learn the continuous and perfect modes of the verb, they can be told that the verbs they first learned were known as the simple tenses. For reference, the table below shows all three modes in past, present and future:

|  | *Past* | *Present* | *Future* |
|---|---|---|---|
| Simple | looked | look | will look |
| Continuous | was looking | is looking | will be looking |
| Perfect | had looked | have looked | will have looked |

Technically there is no future tense in English since, unlike the past tense, the future is not formed by modifying the verb root itself. At this stage, however, it is helpful for the students to think of verbs as taking place in the past, present and future. The complexities are better left until they are older.

Action: The action for verbs is to clench fists and move arms backwards and forwards at sides, as if running.

Color: The color for verbs is red.

## Conjugating verbs: in the present

The students can now learn to conjugate regular verbs. This means saying the pronouns in order, with the correct form of the verb after each. Demonstrate how to conjugate the verb "to run" in the present tense, doing the pronoun actions:

> I run
> you run
> he runs
> she runs
> it runs
> we run
> you run
> they run

Encourage the students to notice how the verb changes after "he," "she" and "it": with regular verbs, an ‹s› is added to the root. This is called the third person singular marker.

Action: The action for the present tense is pointing towards the floor with the palm of the hand.

## Conjugating verbs: in the past

The students need an understanding of what the past is. Initially it helps them to think in terms of what happened yesterday, e.g. "Yesterday I jumped."

The regular past tense is formed by adding the suffix ‹-ed› to the root of the verb. As many verbs have a "tricky" or irregular past form, it is best to choose a regular verb to work with, rather than asking the students for suggestions. Some verbs with regular past tenses are "to jump" (jumped), "to cook" (cooked), "to play" (played). Demonstrate how to conjugate a regular verb in the past tense, doing the pronoun actions:

> I cooked
> you cooked
> he cooked
> she cooked
> it cooked
> we cooked
> you cooked
> they cooked

Write this conjugation on the board, for the students to look at the verbs and see which letters have been added to the root in each case. They can discover for themselves that it is always the suffix ‹-ed›. If the root ends with an ‹e›, as in "bake," this must be removed before the ‹-ed› is added. The ‹-ed› can be pronounced in one of three ways: /t/, as in "slipped," /d/, as in "smiled" or /id/, as in "waited."

Action: The action for the past tense is pointing backwards over the shoulder with a thumb.

Generally, if a verb has a so-called "short vowel" sound, there must be two consonants between the short vowel and the ‹-ed› suffix. If there is only one consonant, this must be doubled. The following list shows examples of some verbs to which the doubling rule applies, and some to which it does not:

*Only one consonant after the short vowel, so doubling rule applies:*

| | | 
|---|---|
| bat | batted |
| hop | hopped |
| pin | pinned |
| rip | ripped |
| hug | hugged |
| trap | trapped |

*No need to double because there are two consonants already:*

| | |
|---|---|
| pick | picked |
| hand | handed |
| rest | rested |
| lift | lifted |
| wish | wished |
| pump | pumped |

The students gradually learn to apply this useful doubling rule.

Although only verbs with regular past tenses are introduced at first, it is not long before the students realize that some verbs have "tricky pasts." They may want to conjugate a verb of their own choosing, such as "to run." It is interesting how quickly some of the students realize that the past tense is not "I runned, you runned," etc. but "I ran, you ran," etc. Those students who are in the habit of regularizing the past tense of irregular verbs in their speech (e.g. saying "I runned") will gradually have to learn the standard irregular forms.

## Conjugating verbs: in the future

The word "yesterday" was used to help the students to understand the idea of the past. Similarly, thinking in terms of "tomorrow" helps them to understand what the future is, e.g. "Tomorrow I shall mail my letter."

With simple verbs, when we speak of future time we use the verb root and add the auxiliary "shall" or "will." "Will" can be used with all the pronouns but "shall" should only be used with "I" and "we," the first person singular and plural. Demonstrate how to conjugate a regular verb in the future, doing the pronoun actions:

> I shall swim
> you will swim
> he will swim
> she will swim
> it will swim
> we shall swim
> you will swim
> they will swim

Action: The action for verbs which describe the future is pointing to the front.

## Adjectives

An adjective is a word that describes a noun or pronoun. At first it is sufficient to tell the students that an adjective describes a noun. Start by asking them to think of a noun, e.g. "a pig." Ask one student for a word to describe it, and say the two together, e.g. "a pink pig." Then ask another student for a second adjective, and add it into the phrase, e.g. "a pink, noisy pig." After several examples the students begin to understand how an adjective functions, especially when used directly before a noun.

When the students begin to apply this knowledge, their stories will become more interesting. Adjectives help the reader to imagine what is taking place.

Action:     The action for an adjective is to touch the side of the temple with a fist.

Color:      The color for adjectives is blue.


## Adverbs

An adverb is similar to an adjective, but describes a verb rather than a noun. Usually adverbs describe how, where, when or how often something happens. They can also be used to modify adjectives or other adverbs, but the students do not need to know this at this stage. Start by asking the students to think of a verb, e.g. "to swim." Ask one student for a word to describe it, and say the two together, e.g. "to swim slowly." (When the verb is in the infinitive form, as here, it is usually better to put the adverb after the root "swim," to avoid a split infinitive, as in "to slowly swim.") After several examples the students begin to understand how an adverb functions. At this stage it helps them to think of an adverb as being found next to a verb, and of often ending with the suffix ‹-ly›. Later, however, the students will discover many instances where this is not the case, and will need to refine their understanding.

Action:     The action for an adverb is to bang one fist on top of the other.

Color:      The color for adverbs is orange.

## a / an / the

The words "a," "an" and "the" are known as articles. "A" and "an" are used before singular nouns and are called the indefinite articles, as in "a person" and "an egg." "The" is used before singular and plural nouns and is called the definite article, as in "the dog" and "the girls." The articles are a special sort of adjective.

Individual schools can decide whether or not to use the full terminology at this stage. While young students like learning new and difficult words, there is a limit to how many they can cope with at once. For most classes it is sufficient to refer to these words as "articles."

The students need to learn when to use "an" instead of "a." As a simple rule of thumb, tell them to look at the word after the article. If the first letter is a vowel, then they should use "an," e.g. "an apple," "an egg," "an itch," "an orange," "an umbrella." There are exceptions to this rule, however, which the students may notice. If a word starts with a "long ⟨u⟩" sound, as in "unicorn" and "union," the article is "a." This is because the "long ⟨u⟩" sound is in fact made up of two sounds, the first of which is the consonant /y/. The same thinking can be applied to words that start with a silent ⟨h⟩. Since the consonant ⟨h⟩ is silent, the first sound that is actually heard is a vowel, so these words take the article "an," e.g. "an hour."

## Sentences

The full definition of a sentence is complicated and more than students can cope with at this stage. However, because they speak in sentences, they already have a general sense of a sentence as expressing a complete thought. If each student is asked for one sentence of news about their weekend, the majority will be able to give one.

At this stage it is sufficient for the students to know that a sentence starts with a capital letter, ends with a period, and must make sense. Soon they will learn that it must also have a verb, and eventually that it must have a subject. Although they are not ready for this yet, it is still important that the students learn about sentences. This knowledge helps them organize their writing into manageable units, rather than linking one idea after another with the word "and."

## Questions

The students need to understand what a question is and how to form a question mark correctly. If a sentence is worded so as to expect an answer, then it is a question and needs a question mark instead of a period. The students need to practice many examples before they remember this automatically. Practice saying sentences and having the students indicate whether or not they are questions. The students can answer by nodding their heads for "yes," or shaking them for "no." Once this exercise becomes familiar the roles can be reversed, with the students thinking up the sentences.

## Parsing: identifying the parts of speech in sentences

Parsing is identifying the function of words in sentences. Each word must be looked at in context to decide which part of speech it is. For example, the sentence "Six girls swam quickly," can be parsed as: adjective, common noun, verb, adverb.

Many words can function as more than one part of speech, e.g. "light" can be the noun "a light," the verb "to light," or the adjective in "a light color." It is only by analyzing a word's use within a sentence that its function can be identified.

The students' ability to parse will develop gradually with regular practice. There are different ways to practice parsing. Start by writing simple sentences on the board for the students to identify the parts of speech. First ask the class, or one student, to read the sentence. Then point to one of the words and ask the students to call out which part of speech it is, or to do the appropriate action. Alternatively, ask individual students to come to the board, and find and underline particular parts of speech in the appropriate colors. Another possibility is to do the action for one of the parts of speech, and call on a student to find an example of it in the sentence and underline it in the appropriate color. Alternatively, have the class copy down the sentence and underline each part of speech in the appropriate color.

# Improving vocabulary and using a dictionary

The speed at which students acquire vocabulary varies enormously. Many students do not do so easily. They have to hear a given word a great many times before adopting it into their vocabulary.

We all use far fewer words in normal speech than we encounter in writing. The more that students read, the greater the likelihood of their vocabulary improving. However, private reading alone is too haphazard a method to rely on, especially for those students without anyone at home who is willing or able to explain the meanings of unfamiliar words.

If a new word is introduced and defined for the students in the classroom, very few are able to recall it or say what it means the following day. To learn the word, most students need to encounter it on several different occasions, practicing saying it and orally putting it into sentences themselves. A systematic approach to vocabulary teaching is therefore very important.

*The Grammar Handbook 1* introduces many words that will be unfamiliar to the students. Obviously the grammatical terms themselves will be new to them. Probably some words from the spelling lists and activity sheets will be too. It is worth choosing a group of words appropriate to the needs of a particular class and teaching them systematically, with enough repetition to ensure that they are mastered.

Young students, who are able to read and to decode new words, are fascinated by dictionaries. Once they are familiar with the alphabet and understand how the dictionary works, they enjoy finding words for themselves. Most students are capable of learning to use a dictionary designed for use in schools. Reading the meanings of the words they find improves the students' comprehension. This is a good habit which should be encouraged; the frequent practice of alphabet and dictionary work in *The Grammar Handbook 1* is designed to help the students acquire it.

When students first begin to write independently, their efforts should be encouraged regardless of the quality. However, after a year of writing freely, the students are ready to learn ways of improving their work. *The Grammar Handbook 1* encourages them to think of alternatives for words they commonly overuse, like "said."

# Teaching ideas for spelling

Most students need to be taught to spell correctly. In *Jolly Grammar*, spelling is the main focus for one lesson each week.

There are a few students who learn to spell well through their reading. These students have a good memory for words. They teach themselves the code of English, mentally noting the different ways the sounds are represented as they read. When they come to write, these students use analogy to think how to spell unfamiliar words. Even when they are unsure of a spelling, they may be able to find it by writing the word in several ways and choosing the correct version. It does not necessarily follow that these students are more intelligent, or produce superior writing. It simply means that they have the necessary combination of attributes for accurate spelling, namely an excellent retentive memory for print, good phonological awareness and strong reasoning skills. When these students are explicitly taught the alphabetic code, they learn even faster.

Just as there are a few students who find it easy to spell accurately, there are some who find it exceedingly difficult. They often have spatial problems, a poor auditory/visual memory, or are inclined to confuse the sequence and direction of letters in words. It is important to identify a student's individual difficulty; whatever the problem, it has to be overcome. These students need a good grasp of phonics, and must recognize the need to work harder and with more self-discipline, if they are to achieve satisfactory results. Parental help is especially important for them.

Most students taught with *Jolly Phonics* in their first school year are familiar with the vowel digraphs and the alternative ways of spelling the vowel sounds, but frequently do not know them by heart. The aim of the spelling work in *Jolly Grammar* is to reinforce the teaching that has gone before, as well as extending the students' knowledge.

*The Grammar Handbook 1* teaches the following spelling features:

- Vowel digraphs,
- Alternative spellings of vowel sounds,
- Plural endings,
- Short vowels and consonant doubling,
- Tricky words, and
- Consonant blends.

These six features are outlined in greater detail in the pages following.

## Vowel digraphs

The students should already be familiar with the blending technique: "If the short vowel sound doesn't work, try the letter name." When reading words with an ‹i› spelling, for example, such as "life," "mind" and "pipe," if the /i/ sound, as in "sit," does not make sense, the students try the /ie/ sound, as in "pie." They can use the same technique with the other four vowels as well, which enables them to decode many unfamiliar words. However, this is a reading technique only, and will not help the students in their writing. For accurate spelling, they need a more thorough understanding of how the vowels work.

"Vowel digraph" is the term for two letters which make a single vowel sound, one or both of the letters being a vowel. Often the two letters are next to each other, e.g. ‹ay›, ‹ea›, ‹ou›, ‹oi›, ‹ew›. Two vowel letters are usually needed to make a so-called "long vowel" sound, i.e. one of the vowel letter names: /ai/, /ee/, /ie/, /oa/ or /ue/. Generally the sound they make is that of the first vowel's name. Hence the well-known rule of thumb "When two vowels go walking, the first does the talking."

Sometimes the long vowel sound is made by two vowels separated by one or more consonants. In monosyllabic words, the second vowel is usually an ‹e›, known as a "magic ‹e›" because it modifies the sound of the first. Digraphs with a "magic ‹e›" can be thought of as "hop-over ‹e›" digraphs: ‹a_e›, ‹e_e›, ‹i_e›, ‹o_e› and ‹u_e›. Once again, the sound they make is that of the first vowel's name; the "magic ‹e›" is silent. Children like to show with a hand how magic from the ‹e› hops over the preceding consonant and changes the short vowel sound to a long one.

This is an alternative way of making the long vowel sounds, as in such words as "bake," "these," "fine," "hope" and "cube." The students need to be shown many examples. It helps them to understand if a piece of paper is held over the ‹e›, and the word is read without it. For example, "ripe" becomes "rip," "hate" becomes "hat," "hope" becomes "hop" and "late" becomes "lat." It does not matter if, as in this last example, the students find themselves producing nonsense words; the exercise will still help them to understand the spelling rule. When looking at texts on the board or in big books, it helps the students to look for and identify words with a "magic ‹e›".

As there are only a few words with the "‹e› hop-over ‹e›" spelling, e.g. "these," "scheme," "complete," and as they are rather rare and usually found in complicated words, this spelling is not taught as one of the main alternatives for the long vowel sounds. However, it is worth introducing it to the class.

## Alternative spellings of vowel sounds

The more complicated aspects of English spelling should be made so familiar to the students that they become automatic. For example, if the students read "The brave woman stayed on the train," they should be able to identify the words with /ai/ sounds: the ‹a_e› in "brave," the ‹ay› in "stayed" and the ‹ai› in "train." By regularly looking for this kind of spelling feature in texts on the board, or in books, the students learn to apply their knowledge in their reading and writing. It is those students who have such knowledge, and know how to use it, who make the greatest progress. It is important that all students acquire these skills. The spellings should be regularly reviewed with flash cards.

In *The Grammar Handbook 1*, the main focus is on the vowel sounds and their alternative spellings. The list below shows the first spelling taught for each letter sound and the main alternatives introduced:

| First spelling taught for sound: | Alternative spellings of sound: | Examples of all spellings in words: |
|---|---|---|
| ai | a_e, ay | rain, came, day |
| ee | ea | street, dream |
| ie | i_e, igh, y | pie, time, light, by |
| oa | o_e, ow | boat, home, snow |
| ue | ew, u_e | cue, few, cube |
| er | ir, ur | her, first, turn |
| oi | oy | boil, toy |
| ou | ow | out, cow |
| ar* | au, aw, al | car, sauce, saw, talk |

* In most regions, ‹ar› makes a slightly different sound from ‹au›, ‹aw› and ‹al›. This difference is reflected in the relevant teacher's lesson notes.

## Plural endings

Plurals are introduced to the students in the grammar lessons. However, there is a direct spin-off into spelling. By recognizing when a word is plural, students can avoid making errors like spelling "ducks" as "dux." Knowing that words ending in ‹sh›, ‹ch›, ‹x›, ‹s› and ‹z› make the plural with an ‹es› ending also helps the students to spell accurately.

## Short vowels and consonant doubling

For almost every rule of spelling in English, there are some words which break it. However, some rules are pretty reliable and make the students' learning easier. One of these is the doubling rule. Hundreds of words follow this rule and very few do not, so it is definitely worth teaching.

Consonant doubling is governed by the short vowels, so the students need to be able to identify short vowel sounds confidently. For an entertaining way of helping them listen for short vowels, a puppet such as the *Inky Mouse puppet* and a box can be used.

> For /a/, put the puppet **a**t the side of the box.
> 
> For /e/, make the puppet wobble on the **e**dge of the box.
> 
> For /i/, put the puppet **i**n the box.
> 
> For /o/, put the puppet **o**n the box.
> 
> For /u/, put the puppet **u**nder the box.

Then the students pretend that their fist is the box and their hand is the puppet.

# Teaching Ideas for Spelling

Start by calling out short vowel sounds. For each one, the students do the appropriate action with their hands. Then call out short words which have a short vowel, e.g. "pot," "hat," "bun," "dig," "red." The students should listen for the vowel sound in each word, and do the action. When most of the students have mastered this, progress to calling out short words with a variety of vowel sounds. For those which do not have a short vowel sound, the students must keep their hands still.

Activities like these help to keep the students "tuned in" to identifying the sounds in words, as well as preparing them for the following rules.

Rules for consonant doubling:

a. In a short (i.e. monosyllabic) word with a short vowel sound, if the last consonant is ‹f›, ‹l›, ‹s› or ‹z›, this is doubled: e.g. "cliff," "bell," "miss," "buzz."

b. In a short word with a short vowel sound, if the last consonant sound is /k/, this is spelled as ‹ck›: e.g. "back," "neck," "lick," "clock," "duck."

c. If there is only one consonant after a short, stressed vowel sound, this consonant is doubled before any suffix starting with a vowel, such as ‹-ed›, ‹-er›, ‹-est›, ‹-ing›, or ‹-y›, as in "hopped," "wetter," "biggest," "clapping" and "funny." Note that when ‹y› is a suffix, it counts as a vowel because it has a vowel sound. (This rule does not apply if the consonant is ‹x›, which is never doubled, even in words like "faxed," "boxing" and "mixer.")

In the case of the suffixes which begin with the letter ‹e›, it helps the students to think of the two consonants as forming a wall. If there were only one consonant, the wall would not be thick enough to prevent "magic" hopping over from the ‹e› and changing the short vowel sound to a long one. With two consonants, the wall becomes so thick that the "magic" cannot get over.

d. When a word ends with the letters ‹le› and the preceding syllable contains a short, stressed vowel sound, there must be two consonants between the short vowel and the ‹le›. This means that the consonant before the ‹le› is doubled in words like "paddle," "kettle," "nibble," "topple" and "snuggle."

No doubling is necessary in words like "handle," "twinkle" and "jungle" because they already have two consonants between the short vowel and the ‹le›.

Young students tend not to grasp rules straight away, but learn them easily if the rules are regularly brought to their attention. As with many skills, success depends on sufficient repetition.

## Tricky Words

The tricky words are a group of keywords which the students need to learn by heart. Most of them have irregular spellings. Although the others are phonically regular, the students need to memorize which spelling of the vowel sound they use. The first sixty tricky words are those introduced in *Jolly Phonics*. These need to be reviewed, and *The Grammar Handbook 1* includes two for review each week. In addition, twelve new tricky words are introduced. A complete list of the seventy-two words is provided on page 194.

## Consonant blends

It is worth devoting time to the consonant blends. They are phonically regular and so provide a reliable guide for both reading and spelling. Review of initial and final consonant blends is provided in the grammar lessons, and each of the weekly spelling lists includes a regular word with a different consonant blend.

The students read unfamiliar words with greater ease once they can blend consonants together fluently, instead of sounding out each one on its own, e.g. "/dr/-/u/-/m/," not "/d/-/r/-/u/-/m/". Flash cards of the blends should be used for regular practice. However, for writing, the students need to be aware of the individual sounds in a blend. They often write a word such as "drum" as "dum" because they do not hear the second sound in the blend. This problem can be overcome with regular practice. Call out blends and ask the students to say the individual sounds, holding up a finger for each one as they say it, e.g. for "dr" they say /d/, /r/ showing two fingers, and for "scr" they say /s/, /c/, /r/," showing three fingers.

# Improving spelling through phonic knowledge

Simply copying words does surprisingly little to improve the students' spelling. For example, some students write the day of the week on all their work by copying from a blackboard or wall chart. Yet even after years of doing so on a daily basis, many still cannot spell the days of the week without copying. If, however, the words are taught in more detail and practiced without copying, the students are quite capable of learning to spell them. Each word needs to be analyzed to see how it is made up, and a technique should be chosen to memorize any irregularities. For the days of the week, for example:

| | |
|---|---|
| Monday | Use the "Say as it sounds" technique, emphasizing the short /o/ so that "Mon" rhymes with "gone." |
| Tuesday | The students listen for, and say the sounds "/T/-/ue/-/s/-/d/-/ay/." Ask them repeatedly how the /oo/ sound is spelled in "Tuesday." |
| Wednesday | Use the "Say it as it sounds" technique, splitting the word into the syllables "Wed-nes-day." |
| Thursday | The students listen for, and say the sounds "/Th/-/ur/-/s/-/d/-/ay/." Ask them repeatedly how the /er/ sound is spelled in "Thursday." |
| Friday | Use the "Say as it sounds" technique, emphasizing the short /i/ so that "Frid" rhymes with "lid." |
| Saturday | Split the word into the syllables "Sat-ur-day." Ask the students repeatedly how the /er/ sound is spelled in "Saturday." |
| Sunday | This is the only day with a perfectly predictable spelling. |

Once the days of the week have been taught, only give the initial letter when writing the date on the board. This encourages the students to practice what they have learned.

In spare moments when looking at texts with students, it helps to look closely at the spelling of some of the words. This develops the students' ability to apply their phonic knowledge to spelling. For example, if the word "circus" comes up, (a) ask why the first ‹c› is soft and has a /s/ sound, (b) ask which spelling of the /er/ sound is used, and (c) point out that saying the last syllable – "us" – as it sounds, helps with remembering the spelling. After a while, this analytic thinking becomes second nature to the students.

*Reproducible Section 1*

# Grammar and Spelling Lesson Sheets

For each lesson there is a reproducible activity sheet for the students to complete, accompanied by a page of teacher's lesson notes. The recommendations in the notes are intended to be followed systematically. However, if a suggestion seems inappropriate to a particular class situation, it can of course be adapted to suit.

All the lesson notes feature a note pad in the top right-hand corner. This shows a brief checklist of what to prepare for teaching, and is intended for easy reference once the teaching notes have been read. (Items which are useful, but not essential, are shown in brackets.)

The **grammar notes** all follow the same format:

a. Objective
b. Introduction
c. Main point
d. Grammar sheet
e. Extension activity
f. Finishing the lesson

Each grammar lesson has its own particular focus, and the teacher's notes vary accordingly. However, the standard format helps to give the lessons a recognizable shape.

# Grammar and Spelling Lesson Sheets

The **spelling notes** also follow a standard format:

a. Review
b. Main point
c. Spelling sheet
d. Dictation
e. Spelling list

Two boxes at the bottom of each page show the words and sentences for dictation, and the weekly spelling list.

Many teaching points are common to all the spelling lessons, so these are explained in further detail below.

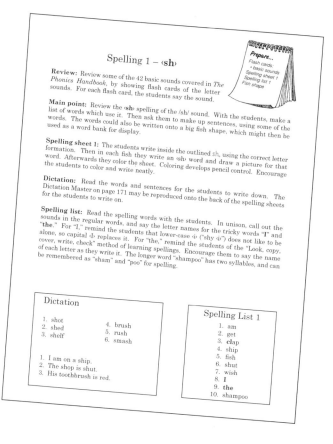

## a. Review

Each lesson should start with a short burst of review. In the early lessons, concentrate on the letter sounds, using flash cards. Over the course of the year, other areas can be added, such as consonant blends, identifying sounds in words, reciting the alphabet, and calling out the letter names of tricky words. The *Jolly Phonics Cards* are useful for this.

## b. Main Point

The main focus of most of the spelling lessons is a digraph, one being featured each week. The students read and sound out words which use the digraph for that week. It is important to have available a set or list of regular words using each of the digraphs. For the /sh/ sound, for example, the list might include "shed," "ship," "wish," "fish," "mesh," "rash" and "splash." Many examples are provided in the *Jolly Phonics Word Book* and the *Jolly Phonics Blending Cards*.

## c. Spelling sheet

The focus of each spelling sheet reflects the main teaching point, whether it is a digraph, a trigraph, or the short vowels. Always encourage the students to be accurate in their work and to color neatly.

## d. Dictation

As a weekly exercise, dictation is useful in a number of ways. It gives the students regular practice in listening for sounds in the words they write, and is a good way of monitoring their progress. It helps the students develop in their independent writing, and encourages the slower writers to increase their speed.

Each dictation list consists of six words and three simple sentences. These all review the spelling introduced that week. For example, if the focus for a particular week is the ‹igh› spelling of the /ie/ sound, then the six dictation words usually feature it.

Begin by calling out the first word for the students to write down. Then ask one of them to sound it out and, as they do so, write the letters on the board. On reaching the sound of the week, the student should say the sound, e.g. /ie/, and then name the letters used to spell it, in this case ‹igh›. The other students see whether they have written the word correctly and, if so, give themselves a check mark. If there is time after the sentences have been dictated, make sure that the regular words in the sentences have been sounded out properly and the tricky words spelled correctly. Have the students say the names of the letters in the tricky words.

Dictation tends to go slowly at first, and it may be necessary to reduce the number of words and sentences. However, aim to go quite fast. When the majority of students have finished a word or sentence, go on to the next. The few students who have not finished should leave the item incomplete, and move on. This encourages them to get up to speed. For extra practice, these students could be given words for dictation homework. (Words may be selected from the Homework Writing Sheets in *The Phonics Handbook*.)

Most of the dictation words are regularly spelled. The students should be able to spell them correctly by listening for each sound and writing the letter(s) for it. This type of teaching helps the students to keep focused on sounds, and prepares them for more advanced work with analogy and word patterns. Most young children are unable to use analogy for reading or spelling until they have been through the phoneme-blending stage and have a reading age of 7+ years.

Without regular practice, some students lose the ability to hear the sounds in words. These tend to be the students who were slowest to acquire phonemic awareness in the first place. It is easy to identify problems by looking at the students' independent writing. For example, if a student writes the word "play" as "paly," this usually indicates that the student needs to be taught to listen more carefully. Regular listening practice is particularly important for such students.

There are a number of activities introduced in *The Phonics Handbook*, which can be used to improve phonemic awareness with a class, group or individual, such as:

- holding up one finger for each sound in a word, e.g. four fingers for "swing,"
- orally "chopping" sounds off a word, one by one, e.g. "spot, pot, ot, t,"
- splitting a word into onset and rime, e.g. "str-eet,"
- splitting a word into syllables, e.g. "luck-y," and
- making new words by changing one sound at a time, e.g. "pin, pip, ship, sheep."

## e. Spelling list

Each week the students are given ten spelling words to learn for a test. It makes sense to give the spelling homework at the beginning of the week, and to test at the end of the week or on the following Monday.

The words have been carefully selected to enable every student to have some success, with the majority achieving a perfect score.

Words 1 and 2 in each spelling list are regular 2- or 3-letter words, and the third is also regular, but with a consonant blend. All the students should be able to spell these correctly by listening for the sounds. Words 4, 5, 6, 7 and 10 generally feature the spelling of the week, and are usually regular. Number 10 is a longer word. The students need encouragement in tackling long words to build their confidence. Words 8 and 9 are tricky words that need to be practiced, by repeating the letter names and by using the "Look, Copy, Cover, Write, Check" method (see pages 195-200). Allow a few minutes each day for reciting the letter names of these two words, especially with the students who normally fail to get a perfect

### Spelling List 1
1. am
2. get
3. **clap**
4. ship
5. fish
6. shut
7. wish
8. **I**
9. **the**
10. shampoo

# GRAMMAR AND SPELLING LESSON SHEETS

score on their spelling homework. It is important to go over the words on the list during the spelling lesson. It is not enough simply to send home a list of words for the students to learn. At odd moments during the week ask the class, or individual students, to spell or sound out words from the list orally, or to test each other in pairs.

Each student takes the spelling list home in a small vocabulary-size exercise book. In Reproducible Section 4 the spelling words are set out in the groups of ten, ready to be copied. At the beginning of each week, paste the right section into each student's Spelling Homework Book. At this stage it is best not to ask the students to write the words into their books themselves, because it is time-consuming, and their writing is not always neat enough for their parents to read.

Test and grade the spelling lists each week. The results should be written in the Spelling Homework Book for the parents to see, shown either as a number right out of ten, or with a coded system if preferred. A colored star system might be used, for example, with a gold star for 10/10, a silver star for 9/10 and a colored star for 8/10. A letter of encouragement to parents is provided on page 187. Most parents like to be involved in the homework, and are interested in how many words their child spelled correctly and which words were misspelled.

Students need to be aware that accurate spelling is important for their future. There is no magic wand that can be waved to make them good at spelling. A certain amount of dedication and practice is needed.

*Jolly Phonics* introduced the students to three spelling techniques:

- "Look, Copy, Cover, Write, Check,"
- "Say as it sounds," and
- Mnemonics.

*Jolly Grammar* continues to encourage the use of these methods. Reproducible sheets for practicing the tricky word spellings with the "Look, Copy, Cover, Write, Check" method are provided on pages 195-200.

# Spelling 1 – ‹sh›

**Review:** Review some of the 42 basic sounds covered in *The Phonics Handbook*, by showing flash cards of the letter sounds. For each flash card, the students say the sound.

**Main point:** Review the ‹sh› spelling of the /sh/ sound. With the students, make a list of words which use it. Then ask them to make up sentences, using some of the words. The words could also be written onto a big fish shape, which might then be used as a word bank for display.

**Spelling sheet 1:** The students write inside the outlined sh, using the correct letter formation. Then in each fish they write an ‹sh› word and draw a picture for that word. Afterwards they color the sheet. Coloring develops pencil control. Encourage the students to color and write neatly.

**Dictation:** Read the words and sentences for the students to write down. The Dictation Master on page 171 may be reproduced onto the back of the spelling sheets for the students to write on.

**Spelling list:** Read the spelling words with the students. In unison, call out the sounds in the regular words, and say the letter names for the tricky words "**I**" and "**the**." For "I," remind the students that lower-case ‹i› ("shy ‹i›") does not like to be alone, so capital ‹I› replaces it. For "the," remind the students of the "Look, copy, cover, write, check" method of learning spellings. Encourage them to say the name of each letter as they write it. The longer word "shampoo" has two syllables, and can be remembered as "sham" and "poo" for spelling.

## Dictation

1. shot
2. shed
3. shelf
4. brush
5. rush
6. smash

1. I am on a ship.
2. The shop is shut.
3. His toothbrush is red.

## Spelling List 1

1. am
2. get
3. **clap**
4. ship
5. fish
6. shut
7. wish
8. **I**
9. **the**
10. shampoo

Write an ‹**sh**› word and draw a picture in each fish.

 **Action:** Place finger over lips and say *sh, sh, sh*.

Spelling sheet 1

# Grammar 1 – Rainbow Capitals

**Objective:** Develop the students' ability to recognize and write capital letters. Develop their knowledge of the alphabet.

Knowing the alphabet is the first step towards being able to use word books, dictionaries and thesauruses.

**Introduction:** Say the alphabet with the students. There should be a copy available that they can see. Point to a letter and ask the students to say its sound. Repeat with other letters. The students need to know the order of the alphabet thoroughly. Throughout this semester they should practice reciting it as often as possible.

**Main point:** Go over the formation of the capital letters. Always start at the top. The starting point for "O" and "Q" is slightly to the right, as if writing a letter "C."

**Grammar sheet 1:** The students write inside the outlined letters, using a colored pencil. Then they have another try, writing the letters with a different colored pencil. Their lines will cross over each other inside the outlines, but this does not matter. The students keep writing the letters, using a different colored pencil each time, until each letter is filled with its own "rainbow."

**Extension activity:** The students put letters into alphabetical order, using the Alphabet Letter Sets on pages 202-3. They could also use any alphabet puzzles available.

**Finishing the lesson:** Give each student a different letter from one of the Alphabet Letter Sets. The students take turns saying the sound and/or name of their letter.

# Rainbow Capital Letters

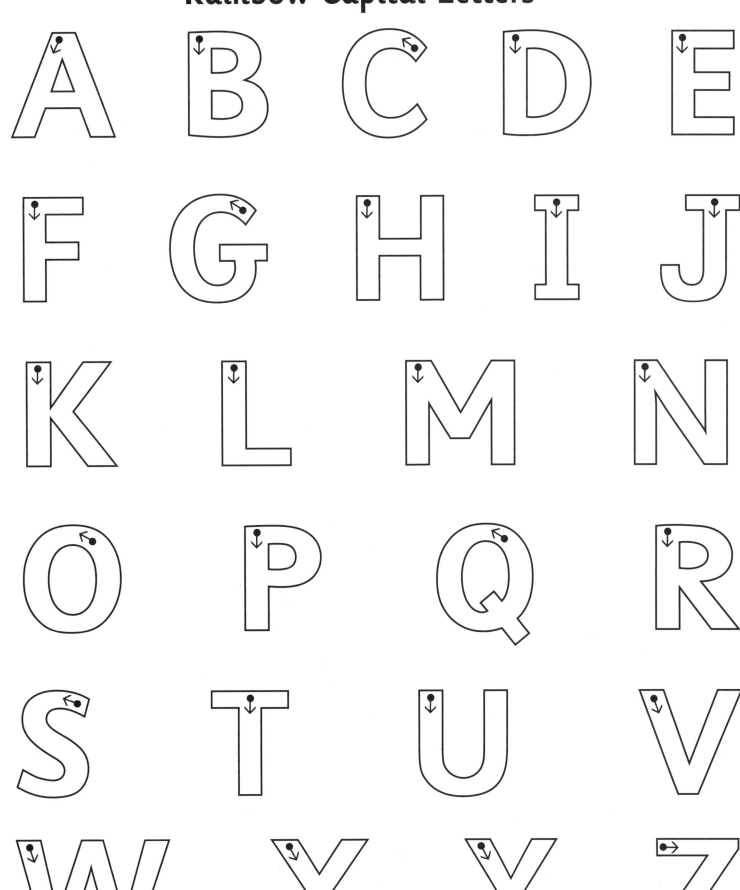

Grammar sheet 1

# Spelling 2 – ‹ch›

**Prepare...**
Flash cards:
• basic sounds
• tricky words
Spelling sheet 2
Spelling list 2
Chest shape

**Review:** Review some basic sounds. Review tricky words "**I**" and "**the**."

**Main point:** Review the ‹ch› spelling of the /ch/ sound. With the students, make a list of words which use it. Then ask them to make up sentences, using some of the words. The words could also be written onto a big chest shape, which might then be used as a word bank for display.

**Spelling sheet 2:** The students write inside the outlined ch, using the correct letter formation. Then in each chest they write a ‹ch› word and draw a picture for that word. Afterwards they color the sheet. Coloring develops pencil control. Encourage the students to color and write neatly.

**Dictation:** Read the words and sentences for the students to write down. The Dictation Master on page 171 may be reproduced onto the back of the spelling sheets for the students to write on.

**Spelling list:** Read the spelling words with the students. In unison, call out the sounds in the regular words, and say the letter names for the tricky words "**he**" and "**she**." The longer word "chicken" has two syllables and can be remembered as "chick" and "en" for spelling. It helps the students remember the spelling if they emphasize the /e/ sound in the second syllable, pronouncing it to rhyme with "pen."

## Dictation

1. chin
2. much
3. chip
4. chimp
5. such
6. lunch

<br>

1. I am rich.
2. She sat on the bench.
3. We chat at lunch.

## Spelling List 2

1. if
2. hot
3. **bl**ot
4. chips
5. lunch
6. chest
7. much
8. **he**
9. **she**
10. chicken

Write a ‹**ch**› word and draw a picture in each chest.

**Action:** Move arms at sides as if you are a train, saying *ch, ch, ch*.

Spelling sheet 2

# Grammar 2 – Sentence pasting

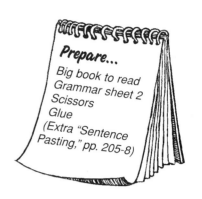

**Objective:** Develop the students' understanding of sentences.

**Introduction:** Explain that sentences help to organize words and to make meaning clear. Read a passage aloud, ignoring all the punctuation. Ask the students what is wrong. Ask them how they know where a sentence begins and ends. Read the passage again with the correct punctuation. Point out the capital letter and period at the beginning and end of each sentence.

**Main point:** Tell the students that sentences help organize both spoken and written words. Ask several students to tell the class one sentence of news each. Choose one of the sentences and write it on the board, without punctuation.

Example:     we went to the park

Ask if this is a sentence, and if not why not. Put in the capital letter and period.

**Grammar sheet 2:** The students need to unscramble the words to make a sentence. Remind them to look for the capital letter to go at the beginning, and the period to go at the end. They can cut the words off the bottom of the sheet and paste them in the correct order into the spaces under the picture. It helps some students to move the words around physically. By cutting the words out and trying to put them in order, these students can be sure they are right before making a final decision. Alternatively the words can simply be written in the correct order in the boxes.

**Extension activity:** There are some more "Sentence Pasting" Sheets on pages 205-8. The students could also write some sentences of their own about the picture. The Writing Master on page 172 may be reproduced onto the back of the grammar sheets for the students to write on.

**Finishing the lesson:** Go over the sheet with the class, so all the students can see if they got the sentence right. If any students have done additional sentence pasting or writing, ask them to share it with the rest of the class.

# Sentences

Cut out the words.
Put them in order, to make a sentence about the picture.

|  |  |  |
|---|---|---|
|  |  |  |

| pond. | A | duck |
|---|---|---|
| on | swims | the |

Grammar sheet 2

# Spelling 3 – ‹th›

**Review:** Review some basic sounds. Review tricky words "I," "the," "he" and "she."

**Main point:** Review the ‹th› spelling of the voiced and unvoiced /th/ sounds. To help the students feel the difference between the voiced and unvoiced sounds, tell them to touch the front of their throats. With a voiced /th/ they will feel vibrations, whereas with an unvoiced /th/ they will not. With the students, make a list of words which use /th/. Then ask them to make up sentences, using some of the words. The words could also be written onto a big thought bubble shape, which might then be used as a word bank for display.

Examples:  voiced /th/:  this  that  then
          unvoiced /th/:  thin  thick  three

**Spelling sheet 3:** The students write inside the outlined th, using the correct letter formation. Then in each thought bubble they write a ‹th› word and draw a picture for that word. Afterwards they color the sheet. Coloring develops pencil control. Encourage the students to color and write neatly.

**Dictation:** Read the words and sentences for the students to write down. The Dictation Master on page 171 may be reproduced onto the back of the spelling sheets for the students to write on.

**Spelling list:** Read the spelling words with the students. In unison, call out the sounds in the regular words, and say the letter names for the tricky words "**me**" and "**we**." The longer word "thinking" has two syllables and can be remembered as "think" and "ing" for spelling.

## Dictation

1. this
2. then
3. with
4. thin
5. think
6. thick

1. That moth is big.
2. He is thin.
3. She cut the cloth.

## Spelling List 3

1. us
2. sad
3. **fl**ag
4. this
5. with
6. that
7. thank
8. **me**
9. **we**
10. thinking

Write a ‹th› word and draw a picture in each thought bubble.

 **Action:** Pretend to be naughty clowns and stick out tongue a little for *th*, and further for *th*.

Spelling sheet 3

# Grammar 3 – Sentences

**Objective:** Develop the students' understanding of sentences.

**Introduction:** Help the students practice saying the alphabet. There should be a copy available that they can see. Once they know it really well they will not need to look. Point to, or hold up letters (both capital and lower-case), and ask for their names and/or sounds. Ask which letter comes after the one being shown. The students find it easier to name this letter than the one which comes before. This is a good activity for any spare moments.

**Main point:** Explain that simply having a capital letter at the beginning of a line of writing, and a period at the end, does not make a sentence. The words in between must make sense too. (This is a very simple working definition of a sentence which young students can understand. As they gain in understanding it can be added to and refined.) Look at some incorrect sentences with the students.

Examples:   the frog is green
            The cat ran up the.

Ask why each line of text is not a proper sentence. Correct them with the class.

**Grammar sheet 3:** The students read each line of text and decide whether it is a proper sentence. If they think it is correct, they copy the sentence underneath. If not they write the sentence correctly underneath.

**Extension activity:** The students practice writing the alphabet using the Alphabet Writing card on page 204.

**Finishing the lesson:** Go over the sheet, with the class deciding if the sentences are correct. If they are not, ask the students why not, and do the corrections with them.

# Are these sentences correct?

Write out each sentence correctly underneath.

1. the dog is spotty.

_____

2. The duck swims on the.

_____

3. I sleep in a bunkbed.

_____

4. i like ham and. eggs

_____

5. They are playing ball.

_____

Grammar sheet 3

# Spelling 4 – ‹ng›

**Prepare...**
Flash cards:
• basic sounds
• tricky words
Spelling sheet 4
Spelling list 4
Enlarged spelling sheet 4

**Review:** Review some basic sounds. Review tricky words "**I**," "**the**," "**he**," "**she**," "**me**" and "**we**."

**Main point:** Review the ‹ng› spelling of the /ng/ sound. Remind the students that it can go with all of the vowels, not just ‹i›. Practice saying "ang," "eng," "ing," "ong" and "ung." With the students, make a list of words which use each spelling. Then ask them to make up sentences, using some of the words. The words could also be written onto an enlarged copy of Spelling sheet 4, which might then be used as a word bank for display.

**Spelling sheet 4:** The students write inside the outlined ng, using the correct letter formation. Then in each ring they write an ‹ng› word and draw a picture for that word. Afterwards they color the sheet. Coloring develops pencil control. Encourage the students to color and write neatly.

**Dictation:** Read the words and sentences for the students to write down. The Dictation Master on page 171 may be reproduced onto the back of the spelling sheets for the students to write on.

**Spelling list:** Read the spelling words with the students. In unison, call out the sounds in the regular words, and say the letter names for tricky words "**be**" and "**was**." For "was," as well as saying the letter names as they write them, the students could use the "Say it as it sounds" spelling method, pronouncing "was" to rhyme with "mass."

---

### Dictation

1. wing
2. song
3. bring
4. fling
5. sung
6. sprang

1. The string was long.
2. She sang a song.
3. He had a sling on his arm.

### Spelling List 4

1. in
2. leg
3. **glad**
4. ring
5. sang
6. strong
7. lung
8. **be**
9. **was**
10. length

Write an ‹ng› word and draw a picture in each ring.

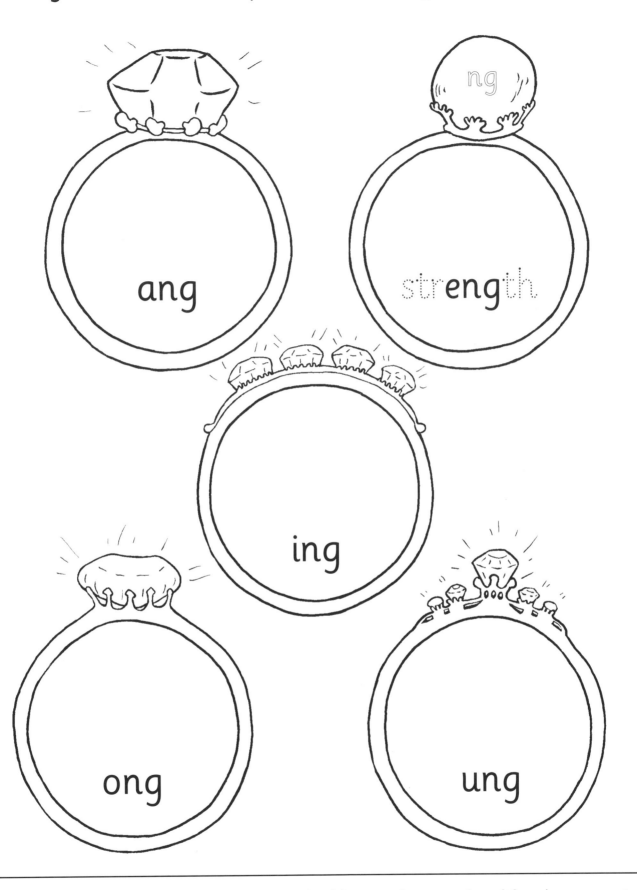

ang

strength

ing

ong

ung

**Action:** Imagine you are a weight lifter and pretend to lift a heavy weight above your head, saying *ng...*

Spelling sheet 4

# Grammar 4 – Capital letters

**Objective:** Develop the students' ability to recognize the capital and lower-case forms of each letter.

**Introduction:** Help the students practice saying the alphabet. There should be a copy available that they can see. Once they know it really well they will not need to look.

**Main point:** Review formation of the capital letters, especially those that are very different from the lower-case letters: ‹A›, ‹B›, ‹D›, ‹E›, ‹F›, ‹G›, ‹H›, ‹M›, ‹N›, ‹Q›, ‹R›, ‹T› and ‹Y›. Write or hold up letters (both capital and lower-case), and ask for their names and/or sounds. Then write or hold up a lower-case letter and ask one of the students to write its capital letter on the board. Repeat with other letters. This is a good activity for spare moments.

**Grammar sheet 4:** The students write the capital letters next to the lower-case letters. Then they join the capital and lower-case letters at the bottom of the sheet.

**Extension activity:** See how quickly the students can sort sets of letters into alphabetical order, using the Alphabet Letter Sets on pages 202-3. The Alphabet Writing Card on page 204 can be used for further practice.

**Finishing the lesson:** From an alphabet set, give each student a different letter. Call out the alphabet slowly. When each letter is called, the student holding it stands up and moves to the front. The students at the front form an alphabet line, holding out their letters for the rest of the class to see. Once all the students come to know the alphabet better, this activity can be repeated with the students saying the names of their letters themselves.

# Capital Letters

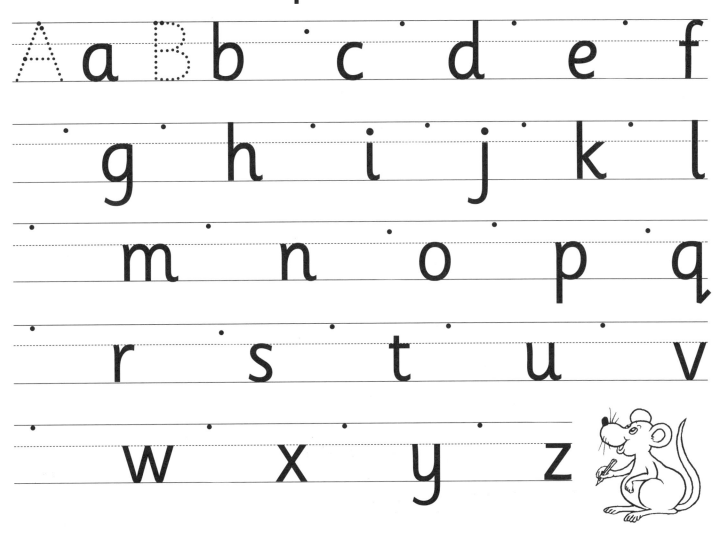

Join each capital letter to its lower-case letter.

Grammar sheet 4

# Spelling 5 – ‹qu›

**Prepare...**
Flash cards:
• basic sounds
• tricky words
Spelling sheet 5
Spelling list 5
Duck shape

**Review:** Review some basic sounds. Review tricky words "**I**," "**the**," "**he**," "**she**," "**me**," "**we**," "**be**" and "**was**."

**Main point:** Review the ‹**qu**› spelling of the /qu/ sound. Remind the students that ‹qu› is made up of two sounds: /k/ and /w/. If the students hear /kw/ in a word, they must remember to write ‹qu›. With the students, make a list of words which use ‹qu›. Then ask them to make up sentences, using some of the words. The words could also be written onto a big duck shape, which might then be used as a word bank for display.

**Spelling sheet 5:** The students write inside the outlined qu, using the correct letter formation. Then in each duck they write a ‹qu› word and draw a picture for that word. Afterwards they color the sheet. Coloring develops pencil control. Encourage the students to write and color neatly.

**Dictation:** Read the words and sentences for the students to write down. The Dictation Master on page 171 may be reproduced onto the back of the spelling sheets for the students to write on.

**Spelling list:** Read the spelling words with the students. In unison, call out the sounds in the regular words, and say the letter names for the tricky words "**to**" and "**do**." At the end of both these words, the letter ‹o› makes an /oo/ sound. The longer word "squirrel" has two syllables and can be remembered as "squir" and "rel" for spelling. It helps the students remember the spelling if they emphasize the /e/ sound in the second syllable, pronouncing it to rhyme with "bell."

## Dictation

1. quit
2. quick
3. quench
4. quail
5. quest
6. liquid

1. She is quick.
2. The ducks say quack.
3. The quiz was on Sunday.

## Spelling List 5

1. on
2. but
3. **pl**um
4. quick
5. quiz
6. queen
7. squid
8. **to**
9. **do**
10. squirrel

Write a ‹qu› word and draw a picture in each duck.

 **Action:** Make a duck's beak with your hands and say *qu, qu, qu*.

Spelling sheet 5

# Grammar 5 – Proper nouns

*Prepare...*
*Story book showing names*
*Jolly Grammar Big Book 1*
*Grammar sheet 5*
*Black pencils*
*(Atlases)*

**Objective:** Develop the students' understanding that there are different types of words, and that each type has a special name.

Proper nouns are the names given to particular people and places, and to months and days of the week.

**Introduction:** The students practice saying the alphabet. Write or hold up capital letters and ask the students to say the name and/or sound for each. Ask some of the students to write their names on the board. Check that they have started their names with a capital letter. Ask the students what all the names on the board have in common. The answer is that they all start with a capital letter. Show the students some names in a story book. Point out that the names all start with a capital letter. Explain that people's names always start with a capital letter.

**Main point:** Special names that are given to people, places or things are called **Proper Nouns**. The students' names are proper nouns. They have a capital letter to show how important they are. Other names are special too and they also need a capital letter, e.g. the name of the school, road, town, state or province, and country. The school address could be written out on a big piece of paper, or "envelope," to be read with the students identifying the proper nouns. The proper nouns should all have capital letters.

- Action: The action for a proper noun is to touch one's forehead with the index and middle fingers.
- Color: The color for nouns is black. (If using a blackboard, explain that as there is no black chalk, white chalk is used instead.)

**Grammar sheet 5:** The students write in the outlined words, Proper Nouns, using a black pencil. Then they draw a picture of themselves in the first frame and write their name underneath, remembering to use a capital letter. There is a space for their last name as well. The students write the name of their teacher under the second frame, and draw a picture in it. Then they write the school address on the picture of the envelope.

**Extension activity:** The students write the names of others at their table, or in their class. They could look for the names of towns and cities in their atlases.

**Finishing the lesson:** Call out words, some of which are proper nouns. For those that are proper nouns, the students do the action. For those that are not, they keep still.

# Proper Nouns 🖉 Black

me

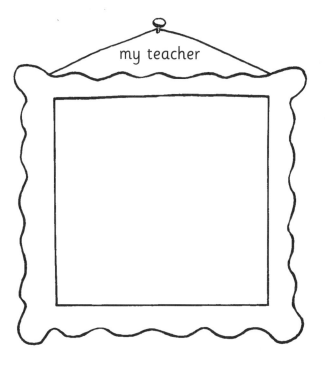

my teacher

_____          _____

_____          _____

**Action:** Touch forehead with index and middle fingers.

**Color:** Black

Grammar sheet 5

# Spelling 6 – ‹or›

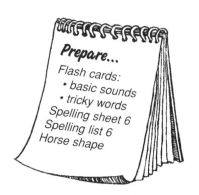

**Review:** Review some basic sounds. Review tricky words "**I**," "**the**," "**he**," "**she**," "**me**," "**we**," "**be**," "**was**," "**to**" and "**do**."

**Main point:** Review the ‹or› spelling of the /or/ sound. With the students, make a list of words which use it. Then ask them to make up sentences, using some of the words. The words could also be written onto a big horse shape, which might then be used as a word bank for display.

**Spelling sheet 6:** The students write inside the outlined or, using the correct letter formation. Then in each horse they write an ‹or› word and draw a picture for that word. Afterwards they color the sheet. Coloring develops pencil control. Encourage the students to color and write neatly.

**Dictation:** Read the words and sentences for the students to write down. The Dictation Master on page 171 may be reproduced onto the back of the spelling sheets for the students to write on.

**Spelling list:** Read the spelling words with the students. In unison, call out the sounds in the regular words, and say the letter names for the tricky words "**are**" and "**all**." Point out to the students that "are" is only tricky because they must remember to put the ‹e› on the end. The longer word "morning" has two syllables and can be remembered as "morn" and "ing" for spelling.

### Dictation

1. corn
2. sort
3. worn
4. torch
5. for
6. sport

1. We cut the corn.
2. She is good at sports.
3. There was a storm this morning.

### Spelling List 6

1. at
2. yes
3. **slug**
4. fork
5. storm
6. horse
7. forty
8. **are**
9. **all**
10. morning

Write an ‹**or**› word and draw a picture in each horse.

 **Action:** Put hands on head as if donkey's ears pointing down, and say *or*. (This comes from the *ee or* action.)

Spelling sheet 6

# Grammar 6 – Common nouns

**Objective:** Develop the students' understanding of common nouns.

**Introduction:** Review proper nouns with the class. Call out some words. For those that are proper nouns, the students do the action. Remind them that proper nouns need a capital letter at the beginning because they are important names.

**Main point:** Tell the students that not all names are important. The word "chair" is a noun but it is not a proper noun. There are many chairs, not just one chair. These sorts of nouns are **Common Nouns**, and do not need capital letters. If it makes sense to put "a," "an" (the indefinite articles) or "the" (the definite article) in front of a word, then the word is probably a noun. It may help the students' understanding to tell them that nouns are things that can be photographed. However, this is true only of concrete nouns, and not of abstract nouns such as "happiness."

- Action: The action for a common noun is to touch one's forehead with all the fingers of one hand.
- Color: The color for nouns is black. (If using a blackboard, explain that as there is no black chalk, white chalk is used instead.)

Call out some words. The students do the action for those that are common nouns.

**Grammar sheet 6:** The students write inside the outlined words, Common Nouns, using a black pencil. Then, in each "photograph," the students draw an object or animal. It may help them to look around and choose three things that they can see. The students write the common noun for each picture underneath it. In the next exercise, they read the sentences and write a noun that makes sense in each space. Then they draw pictures for their nouns in the "photograph" frames.

**Extension activity:** The students write nouns and draw pictures for other things they can see around them. They can pretend to have a camera, and look around for things to photograph.

**Finishing the lesson:** Call out words including some proper nouns and some common nouns. For words that are proper or common nouns, the students do the appropriate action. For words that are neither, they keep still.

# Common Nouns

Draw 3 pictures and write nouns for them underneath.

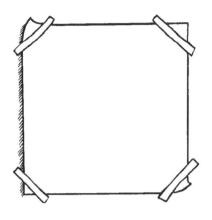  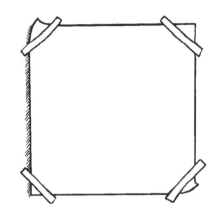  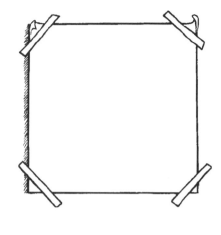

_____   _____   _____

Write a noun to finish each sentence, and draw a picture.

1. The _____ is black.

2. I throw the _____ .

3. A _____ can swim.

4. I like to eat _____ .

---

**Action:** Put hand on forehead.

**Color:** Black

Grammar sheet 6

# Spelling 7 – **short vowels**

**Prepare...**
Flash cards:
Jolly Grammar
Big Book 1
(Inky Mouse puppet and box)
Spelling sheet 7
Spelling list 7

**Review:** Review some basic sounds. Review tricky words "**he**," "**she**," "**me**," "**we**," "**be**," "**was**," "**to**," "**do**," "**are**" and "**all**."

**Main point:** Review the short vowel sounds: /**a**/, /**e**/, /**i**/, /**o**/, /**u**/. The students can "count" them on their fingers, starting with the thumb for /a/. Many spelling rules relate to the short vowel sounds. The students need to be able to identify the vowel sounds in words, and to know which ones are short. Use a box and puppet (the *Inky Mouse puppet* if possible) to help them listen for the short vowel sounds:

> For /a/, put the puppet <u>a</u>t the side of the box. For /e/, make the puppet wobble on the <u>e</u>dge of the box. For /i/, put the puppet <u>i</u>n the box. For /o/, put the puppet <u>o</u>n the box. For /u/, put the puppet <u>u</u>nder the box.

The students make a fist with one hand. They pretend that this is the box and that their other hand is Inky mouse. Call out the short vowel sounds for them to put their mouse hand <u>a</u>t, on the <u>e</u>dge of, <u>i</u>n, <u>o</u>n or <u>u</u>nder their fist, as appropriate. (See pictures on page 17.)

**Spelling sheet 7:** Call out words with short vowel sounds. The students practice identifying the vowel sound and saying where Inky should go, e.g. "cat" has a short /a/ sound so Inky goes <u>a</u>t the side. For each word on Spelling sheet 7, the students identify its short vowel sound, find a box with that sound, and copy it into the box.

**Dictation:** Read the words and sentences for the students to write down. The Dictation Master on page 171 may be reproduced onto the back of the spelling sheets.

**Spelling list:** Read the spelling words with the students. This week's list is different, as it features four days of the week. The others are in the next list. In unison, say the letter names for the tricky words "**you**" and "**your**." The longer word "yesterday" has three syllables and can be remembered as "yes," "ter" and "day."

## Dictation

1. bat
2. bug
3. pin
4. flag
5. drop
6. send

<br>

1. I sat on a bench.
2. She had a bad cut.
3. That was a big bang.

## Spelling List 7

1. it
2. dog
3. **br**an
4. Monday
5. Tuesday
6. Wednesday
7. Thursday
8. **you**
9. **your**
10. yesterday

# Short Vowel Sounds

Write each word into a box with the same short vowel sound.

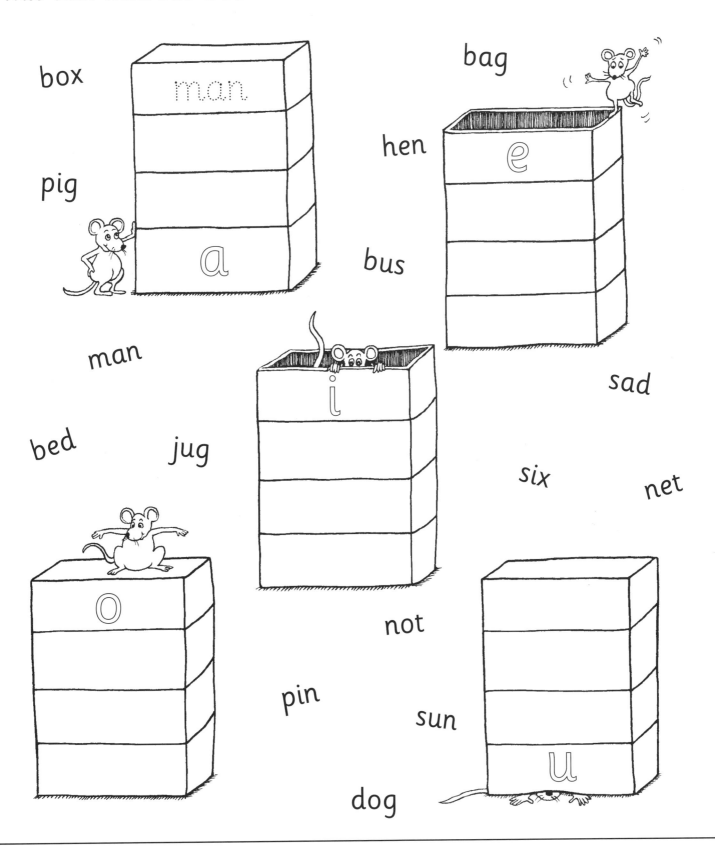

Aa  Ee  Ii  Oo  Uu

Spelling sheet 7

# Grammar 7 – Alphabetical order

**Prepare...**
Alphabet in four groups (Dictionary)
Grammar sheet 7
Colored pencils (Alphabet Letter Sets, pp. 202-3)

**Objective:** Develop the students' knowledge of the alphabet.

**Introduction:** The students need to be thoroughly familiar with each letter's position in the alphabet and dictionary. This will improve their ability to find words in the dictionary. Show the students a dictionary and explain what it is for. Tell the students that if a dictionary were divided into four approximately-equal parts, the letters would fall into the following groups:

1. Aa Bb Cc Dd Ee
2. Ff Gg Hh Ii Jj Kk Ll Mm
3. Nn Oo Pp Qq Rr Ss
4. Tt Uu Vv Ww Xx Yy Zz

The students practice saying the alphabet in these groups. They hold up one finger as they say the first group, pause, then hold up two fingers as they say the second, etc. A copy of the alphabet divided into the four groups should be available for them to see.

**Main point:** Point to, or hold up letters (both capital and lower-case), and ask for their names and/or sounds. Ask which letter comes after the one being shown, and which comes before it. This activity is ideal for any spare moments, and needs to be repeated often for the students to learn the alphabet thoroughly.

**Grammar sheet 7:** Using a different colored pencil for each group, the students write inside the outlined lower-case letters. Then they write the capital letters next to the lower-case ones. Next they write the letters that come before and after those in each group of books. Finally they try putting groups of letters into alphabetical order. The letters in each group of three are consecutive, and should be written as capitals.

**Extension activity:** Put more letters on the board, or letter cards on tables, for the students to put into alphabetical order.

**Finishing the lesson:** Give each student a different letter from one of the Alphabet Letter Sets on pages 202-3. Call out a letter. The student with that letter stands up. Then ask who has the letter that comes after it, and who has the letter that comes before. The students stand next to each other holding their letters in front of them.

# Alphabetical Order

Use a different color for each section of the alphabet.
Write the capital letters next to the lower-case letters.

__a __b __c __d __e
__f __g __h __i __j __k __l __m
__n __o __p __q __r __s
__t __u __v __w __x __y __z

Which letters come before and after?

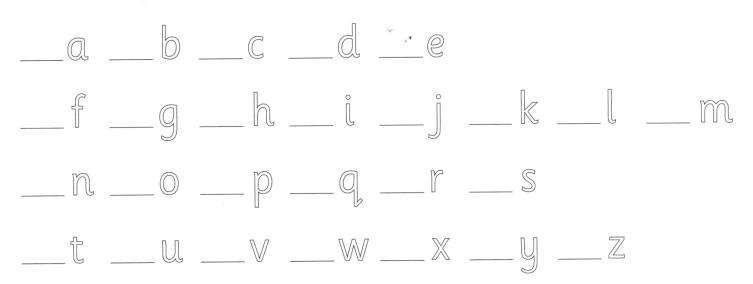

Put these sets of letters into alphabetical order.

| C A B | M L K | U V T |
|---|---|---|
| ___ ___ ___ | ___ ___ ___ | ___ ___ ___ |

Grammar sheet 7

# Spelling 8 – short vowels

**Review:** Review some basic sounds. Review tricky words "**me**," "**we**," "**be**," "**was**," "**to**," "**do**," "**are**," "**all**," "**you**" and "**your**."

**Main point:** Review the short vowels, /**a**/, /**e**/, /**i**/, /**o**/, /**u**/, using the actions for Inky and the box (see Spelling 7). Many spelling rules relate to the short vowel sounds, so students need to be able to identify them in words. Set out five containers, a b**a**g, n**e**t, b**i**n, b**o**x, and m**u**g, as on the sheet. Call out a word and ask the students to say which short vowel sound it contains, and to decide which container has the corresponding vowel sound, i.e. /a/ words go into the bag, and /e/ words into the net, etc. If the containers suggested are not available, an enlarged copy of the sheet could be used, or boxes could be labelled with the vowel letters.

**Spelling sheet 8:** Spelling sheet 8 can be used in any of the following ways:
a) Call out words for the students to write into the appropriate containers.
b) Put a selection of consonant/vowel/consonant word cards on each table. The students read the words and then write them into the appropriate containers. Ensure that there are at least three words for each vowel sound.
c) Tell the students to think of three words with an /a/ sound, and write them in the bag, then three words with an /e/ sound, to be written in the net, etc.

**Dictation:** Read the words and sentences for the students to write down. The Dictation Master on page 171 may be reproduced onto the back of the spelling sheets.

**Spelling list:** Read the spelling words with the students. The remaining days of the week are introduced. The students need to learn to spell them accurately. From next week, try putting only the initial letter on the board when writing the date, so that students have to complete the word from memory. In unison, say the letter names for the tricky words "**come**" and "**some**." The longer word "weekend" has two syllables and can be remembered as "week" and "end" for spelling.

## Dictation

1. Sunday
2. Monday
3. Tuesday
4. Wednesday
5. Thursday
6. week

1. It is Monday.
2. Yesterday was Sunday.
3. I swim on Thursdays.

## Spelling List 8

1. up
2. man
3. **cr**ab
4. Friday
5. Saturday
6. Sunday
7. today
8. **come**
9. **some**
10. weekend

# Short Vowel Sounds

Think of some words for each short vowel sound and write them in the right container.

Aa  Ee  Ii  Oo  Uu

Spelling sheet 8

# Grammar 8 – "a" or "an"

**Objective:** Develop the students' knowledge of when to use "an" instead of "a." ("A" and "an" are the indefinite articles.)

**Introduction:** Review the five vowel letters. Tell the students that all the other letters are called consonants. Review the short vowel sounds /a/, /e/, /i/, /o/, /u/. Review the actions for them, using Inky mouse and the box, as on Spelling 7. Call out some consonant/short vowel/consonant words. For each word, the students listen for the short vowel sound and do the appropriate action.

**Main point:** Write the following sentences on the board, and read them with the class. Ask the students to help identify and underline the nouns. Ask what is wrong with the sentences, and correct them.

Sentences: An shark has an fin.
They saw a elephant at the zoo.

Explain that usually if a noun starts with a vowel sound we use "an," and if it starts with a consonant we use "a." If it makes sense to put "a," "an" or the definite article "the" before a word, then the word is probably a noun. Call out nouns, some of which begin with a vowel, for the students to decide whether to use "a" or "an."

**Grammar sheet 8:** Go over the sheet with the students, asking what each picture shows. If necessary, sound out and write the words on the board. The students can either just write "a" or "an" underneath each picture, or they can write the noun for the picture as well.

**Extension activity:** The students write down as many nouns as they can that begin with a vowel. They could use a dictionary to help them. The Writing Master on page 172 may be reproduced onto the back of the grammar sheets for the students to write on.

**Finishing the lesson:** Go over the sheet with the class. Then ask each student for a word beginning with a vowel.

# a or an?

Write "an" for each word beginning with a vowel, and "a" for the others.

_____

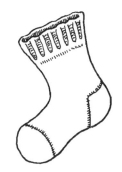
_____

_____

_____

_____

_____

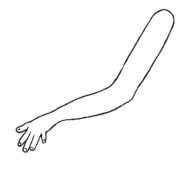
_____

_____

_____

Aa   Ee   Ii   Oo   Uu

Grammar sheet 8

# Spelling 9 – ‹ff›

**Review:** Review some basic sounds. Review tricky words "**be**," "**was**," "**to**," "**do**," "**are**," "**all**," "**you**," "**your**," "**come**" and "**some**."

**Main point:** Introduce the ‹**ff**› spelling of the /f/ sound. At the end of a small word with a short vowel, ‹f› is usually doubled, except in the words "if" and "of." Explain to the students that they can remember the difference between "of" and "off," by listening to the sound at the end of the word. If it is a /f/ sound, as in "off," then they must use ‹ff›, but if they hear a /v/ sound, as in "of," they only need one ‹f›. With the students, make a list of words which use ‹ff›. Then ask them to make up sentences, using some of the words. The words could also be written onto a big cliff shape.

**Spelling sheet 8:** The students write inside the outlined ff. Then in each cliff they write an ‹ff› word and draw a picture for that word. Afterwards they color the sheet.

**Dictation:** Read the words and sentences for the students to write down. The Dictation Master on page 171 may be reproduced onto the back of the spelling sheets for the students to write on.

**Spelling list:** Read the spelling words with the students. In unison, call out the sounds in the regular words, and say the letter names for the tricky words "**said**" and "**here**." The longer word "puffin" has two syllables and can be remembered as "puf" and "fin" for spelling.

## Dictation

1. off
2. cuff
3. huff
4. gruff
5. ruff
6. cliff

1. He can jump off the step.
2. She ran up the cliff.
3. We sniff the buds.

## Spelling List 9

1. red
2. win
3. **drum**
4. off
5. cliff
6. stiff
7. cuff
8. **said**
9. **here**
10. puffin

Write an ‹**ff**› word and draw a picture on each cliff.

cliff

**Action:** Let hands gently come together as if fish deflating and say *ffffff*.

Spelling sheet 9

# Grammar 9 – Plurals

**Objective:** Develop the students' understanding of singular and plural, and their knowledge that the simplest way to make the plural of a word is to add ‹s›.

**Introduction:** Hide any copies of the alphabet. Sit the students in a circle, and ask one student to say the first letter of the alphabet. Go round the circle, with each student saying the next letter. Repeat this, choosing a different student to start each time, so that the students do not always say the same letter.

**Main point:** Hold up a picture of a dog and ask the students what it shows. Then hold up a picture of several dogs, and ask what this picture shows. Write "dog" and "dogs" on the board. Ask the students how the two words differ. Explain that nouns usually change when they describe more than one. The name for nouns which describe one of something is **singular**, and the name for nouns which describe more than one is **plural**. The simplest way of making a plural is by adding an ‹s› to the end of the noun. Call out examples of singular nouns and ask the students to give plurals for them, e.g. for "one cat" they say "lots of cat**s**." Only call out nouns which have regular plurals.

| Examples: | cat | rat | flag | hen | ant | pig | tree | bird |
|---|---|---|---|---|---|---|---|---|
| | bun | bed | drum | pen | map | leg | doll | van |
| | cloud | duck | bat | car | boat | | | |

**Grammar sheet 9:** The students read each noun and decide whether it is singular or plural. They draw a picture for each, remembering that for plural nouns they must draw more than one item. Then they look at the pictures in the boxes underneath. They write the noun for each picture, remembering that if it shows more than one item, they must add an ‹s› to make the plural.

**Extension activity:** The students could do the "Pull-Out Plurals" Sheet on page 209.

**Finishing the lesson:** Go over the sheet with the class, checking which nouns are plural and which are singular.

# Plurals

Draw a picture for each word.

|   |   |   |
|---|---|---|
|   |   |   |
| hats | pens | dog |

|   |   |   |
|---|---|---|
|   |   |   |
| cars | cow | frog |

Write the word for each picture.

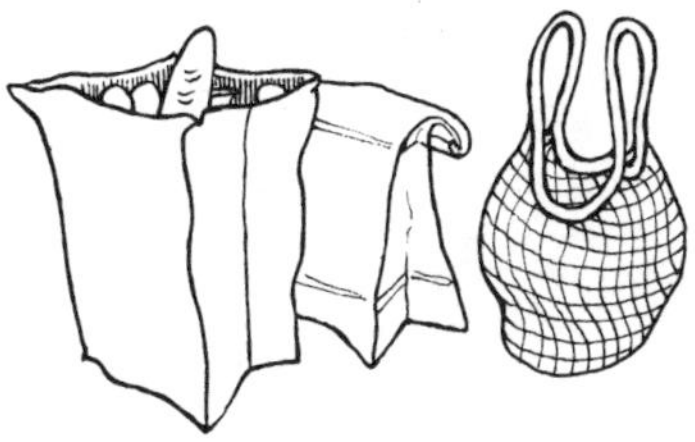

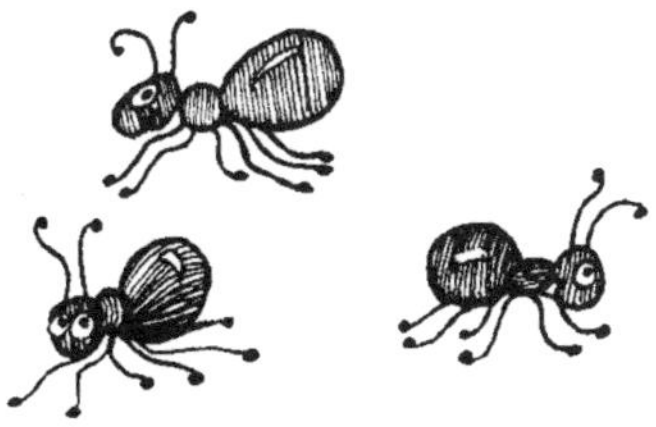

_____  _____  _____

_____  _____  _____

Grammar sheet 9

# Spelling 10 – ⟨ll⟩

**Review:** Review some basic sounds and ⟨ff⟩. Review tricky words "**to**," "**do**," "**are**," "**all**," "**you**," "**your**," "**come**," "**some**," "**said**" and "**here**."

**Main point:** Introduce the ⟨ll⟩ spelling of the /l/ sound. At the end of a small word with a short vowel, ⟨l⟩ is usually doubled. With the students, make a list of words which use ⟨ll⟩. Then ask them to make up sentences, using some of the words. The words could also be written onto a big bell shape.

**Spelling sheet 10:** The students write inside the outlined ll. Then in each bell they write an ⟨ll⟩ word and draw a picture for that word. Afterwards they color the sheet.

**Dictation:** Read the words and sentences for the students to write down. The Dictation Master on page 171 may be reproduced onto the back of the spelling sheets for the students to write on.

**Spelling list:** Read the spelling words with the students. In unison, call out the sounds in the regular words, and say the letter names for the tricky words "**there**" and "**they**." For "there," ask the students to look for the word "here" inside it. The longer word "windmill" has two syllables and can be remembered as "wind" and "mill" for spelling.

| Dictation | Spelling List 10 |
|---|---|
| 1. ill    4. doll | 1. ox |
| 2. tell   5. smell | 2. run |
| 3. gull   6. drill | 3. **from** |
|  | 4. will |
| 1. You must tell your Mom. | 5. bell |
| 2. She fell ill. | 6. doll |
| 3. He can spell well. | 7. skull |
|  | 8. **there** |
|  | 9. **they** |
|  | 10. windmill |

Write an ‹ll› word and draw a picture in each bell.

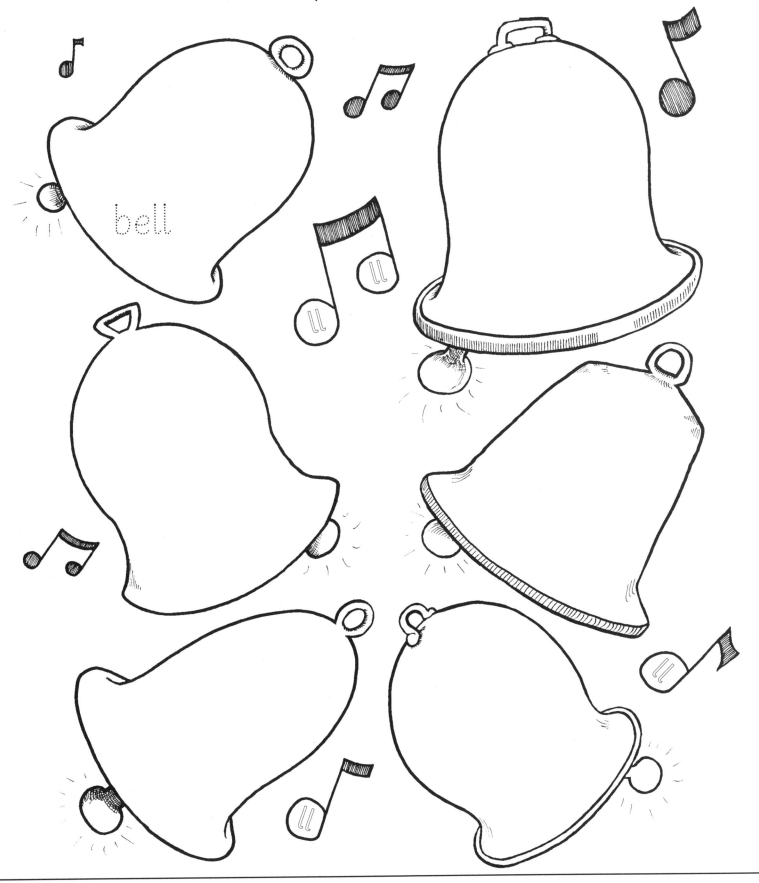

 **Action:** Pretend to lick a lollipop and say l, l, l, l.

# Grammar 10 – Pronouns

Prepare...
Jolly Grammar Big Book 1
Grammar sheet 10
Pink pencils

**Objective:** Develop the students' knowledge of personal pronouns.

**Introduction:** Tell the students a story without using any personal pronouns.

Example: "Mark was having a birthday party. Mark wanted to blow up some balloons. Mark blew too hard and burst one of the balloons. His sister laughed. His sister helped Mark to blow up some more balloons."

Ask the students why the story sounds wrong.

**Main point:** Explain that to avoid continually repeating the same nouns, we use other, short words to take their place. These short words are called **pronouns**. Pronouns take the place of nouns. Check that the students remember what a noun is. Tell the students the personal pronouns. There is an action for each one:

Actions:
- I – point to self
- you – point to someone else
- he – point to a boy
- she – point to a girl
- it – point to the floor
- we – point in a circle to include self and others
- you – point to two other people
- they – point to the next-door class

Color: The color for pronouns is pink.

Tell the students that the words "we" and "they" are plural. The word "you" appears twice. Make sure the students understand that it is singular the first time and plural the second. This will help them when they begin to learn other languages.

**Grammar sheet 10:** The students write inside the outlined word, Pronouns, in pink. Then they write inside all the outlined pronouns in pink. They read the pronouns and draw pictures for them. For "I," the students draw themselves. If the pronoun is plural they must draw more than one person.

**Extension activity:** The students could write a sentence for each pronoun. The Writing Master on page 172 may be reproduced onto the back of the grammar sheets for the students to write on.

**Finishing the lesson:** Go over the actions with the class.

# Pronouns  Pink

Color the pronouns pink. Draw a picture for each pronoun. Remember which are singular and which are plural.

Grammar sheet 10

# Spelling 11 – ‹ss› / ‹zz›

**Review:** Review some basic sounds and the spellings covered so far. Review tricky words "**are**," "**all**," "**you**," "**your**," "**come**," "**some**," "**said**," "**here**," "**there**" and "**they**."

**Main point:** Introduce the ‹ss› spelling of the /s/ sound, and the ‹zz› spelling of the /z/ sound. At the end of a small word with a short vowel, ‹s› and ‹z› are usually doubled. There are very few words with the ‹zz› spelling, which is why it is included here with ‹ss›. With the students, make a list of words which use ‹ss› and ‹zz›. Then ask them to make up sentences, using some of the words. The words could also be written onto a big dress shape, with a bee shape drawn on it for the ‹zz› words.

**Spelling sheet 11:** The students write inside the outlined ss and zz. Then they write an ‹ss› word in each dress and a ‹zz› word in the bee, and draw a picture for each word. Afterwards they color the sheet.

**Dictation:** Read the words and sentences for the students to write down. The Dictation Master on page 171 may be reproduced onto the back of the spelling sheets for the students to write on.

**Spelling list:** Read the spelling words with the students. In unison, call out the sounds in the regular words, and say the letter names for the tricky words "**go**" and "**no**." The longer word "classroom" has two syllables and can be remembered as "class" and "room" for spelling.

## Dictation

1. hiss
2. buzz
3. fuss
4. jazz
5. cross
6. press

1. You can floss your teeth.
2. She will press the buzzer.
3. I shall miss you.

## Spelling List 11

1. hop
2. fit
3. **grin**
4. buzz
5. cross
6. less
7. miss
8. **go**
9. **no**
10. classroom

Write an ‹ss› word in each dress and a ‹zz› word in the bee.
Draw a picture for each word.

 **Action:** Weave hand in an s shape, like a snake, and say *sssssss*.

 **Action:** Put arms out at sides and pretend to be a bee saying *zzzzzzzzzz*.

Spelling sheet 11

# Grammar 11 – Initial blends wheel

**Objective:** Develop the students' awareness of initial consonant blends for reading and writing.

**Introduction:** Students will read words with consonant blends more easily if they are familiar with them, and can blend them almost automatically, e.g. "/dr/-/u/-/m/" rather than "/d/-/r/-/u/-/m/." The individual consonant sounds are not always easy to hear in blends, so knowing them also helps with writing. Call out examples of words containing initial consonant blends, and ask the students to sound them out. Often the students will sound them out using the blend. Ask which sounds are in the blend. Tell the students to hold up one finger for each sound.

| Examples: | flag | press | slip | stop | drum |
|---|---|---|---|---|---|
| | clap | glen | crib | frog | slug |
| | glad | green | swim | prod | club |

**Main point:** Use the Consonant Blends Flash Cards on pages 181-85 to practice reading consonant blends with the class. First hold up the cards and ask the students to say the sound the blend makes, e.g. /fr/, /gl/, /sm/. Then go through the cards again, saying each blend for the students, without letting them see the card. Ask them to say the two sounds that make up each blend. They should count each sound on their fingers.

**Grammar sheet 11:** The students cut out the two discs. The smaller disc is placed on top of the larger one and a split pin is used to fasten them together. They can be strengthened if they are pasted onto card or thick paper before being pinned together. The students turn the discs around and blend the letters to see how many words they can make.

**Extension activity:** The students write a list of all the words they have found.

**Finishing the lesson:** Go round the class, asking each student for one word. Hopefully there will be plenty of different words.

# Initial Blends Wheel

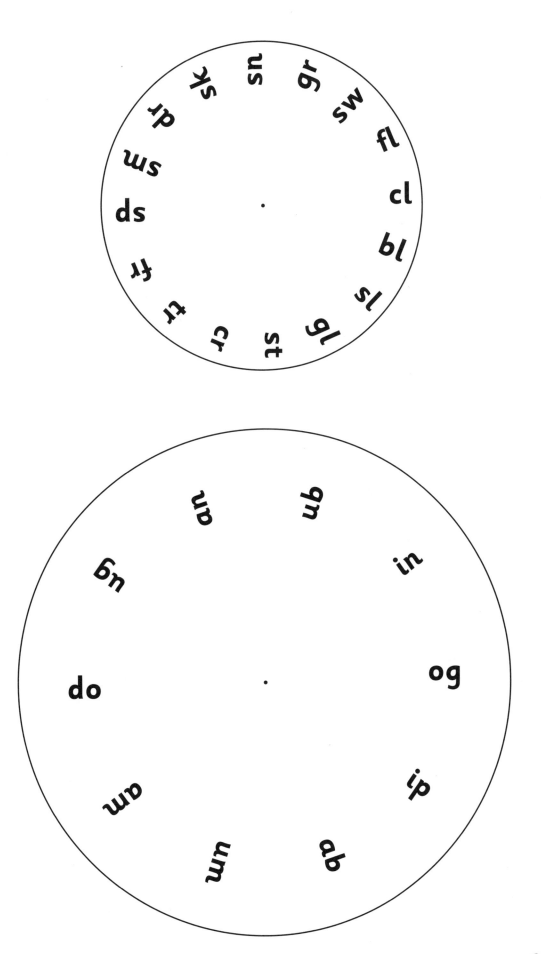

Grammar sheet 11

# Spelling 12 – ‹ck›

**Review:** Review some basic sounds and the other spellings covered so far. Review tricky words "**you**," "**your**," "**come**," "**some**," "**said**," "**here**," "**there**," "**they**," "**go**" and "**no**."

**Main point:** Review the ‹ck› spelling of the hard /c/ sound. At the end of a small word with a short vowel, a ‹c› is usually doubled by adding a "kicking ‹k›." With the students, make a list of words which use ‹ck›. Then ask them to make up sentences, using some of the words. The words could also be written onto a big chick shape.

**Spelling sheet 12:** The students write inside the outlined ck. Then in each chick they write a ‹ck› word and draw a picture for that word. Afterwards they color the sheet.

**Dictation:** Read the words and sentences for the students to write down. The Dictation Master on page 171 may be reproduced onto the back of the spelling sheets for the students to write on.

**Spelling list:** Read the spelling words with the students. In unison, call out the sounds in the regular words, and say the letter names for the tricky words "**so**" and "**my**." In "my" the ‹y› is taking the place of "shy ‹i›." The longer word "backpack" has two syllables and can be remembered as "back" and "pack" for spelling.

### Dictation

1. pack
2. luck
3. peck
4. brick
5. block
6. truck

1. Pack your bag.
2. The boys had a quick snack.
3. This will bring you luck.

### Spelling List 12

1. bed
2. wet
3. **pr**od
4. duck
5. neck
6. clock
7. lick
8. **so**
9. **my**
10. backpack

**Write a ‹ck› word and draw a picture in each chick.**

 **Action:** Raise hand and snap fingers as if playing castanets and say *ck, ck, ck.*

Spelling sheet 12

# Grammar 12 – Initial blends

**Objective:** Develop the students' awareness of initial consonant blends for reading and writing.

**Introduction:** Help the students practice saying the alphabet in the four groups. There should be a copy available for them to see. Ask them to find the vowels. Then ask what all the other letters are called. Hold up flash cards with consonant blends for the students to read.

**Main point:** Call out some consonant blends (see Grammar 11) and ask the students to say which sounds they would need to spell them. The students hold up one finger for each sound they say. Ask them for examples of words starting with each of the blends.

**Grammar sheet 12:** Go over the sheet with the students and ask what each picture shows. The first six pictures use words that are on the "initial blends wheels." The words for the other six pictures are not on the wheels, but the students can use the blends on the inner disc to help them.

(Answers:  
| | | | |
|---|---|---|---|
| | grin | frog | drum |
| | crab | clam | slug |
| | flag | tree | star |
| | snail | swing | spoon) |

**Extension activity:** Write some initial consonant blends on the board, e.g. ‹fl›, ‹sl›, ‹gr›, and ask the students to think of, or find, as many words as possible beginning with each blend.

**Finishing the lesson:** Go over the sheet, with the class sounding out each word.

# Initial Blends

Write the word for each picture.

Use your initial blends wheel to help you.

g r i n

_ _ _ _ _      _ _ _ _ _

_ _ _ _ _      _ _ _ _ _      _ _ _ _ _

These words are not on your wheel but you can use the initial blends on the inner circle to help you.

_ _ _ _ _      _ _ _ _ _      _ _ _ _ _

_ _ _ _ _      _ _ _ _ _      _ _ _ _ _

Grammar sheet 12

# Spelling 13 – **vowels**

**Review:** Review some basic sounds and the other spellings covered so far. Review tricky words "**come**," "**some**," "**said**," "**here**," "**there**," "**they**," "**go**," "**no**," "**so**" and "**my**."

**Main point:** Review the short vowel sounds /a/, /e/, /i/, /o/ and /u/. Vowel letters are different from consonants because they can use their names in words – /ai/, /ee/, /ie/, /oa/ and /ue/ – as well as their sounds. There are also other vowel sounds, besides the sounds and names of the five vowel letters. Digraphs with at least one vowel letter, e.g. ‹oi›, ‹ou›, ‹er› and ‹oo›, also make vowel sounds. Tell the students that all words in English must have at least one vowel sound. Call out some words. If a word contains a short vowel sound, the students do the action to show whether Inky is <u>a</u>t, on the <u>e</u>dge of, <u>i</u>n, <u>o</u>n or <u>u</u>nder the box (see picture on page 17). If not they put their hands in their laps.

**Spelling sheet 13:** The students read the words in the leaves. If a word has a short vowel sound they color its leaf edge yellow. When they have found all the short vowel words they could color the remaining leaf edges green. (The colors can be altered to suit.) When the students have completed the sheet, read through the words, with the class identifying which have short vowel sounds and which do not.

**Dictation:** Read the words and sentences for the students to write down. The Dictation Master on page 171 may be reproduced onto the back of the spelling sheets for the students to write on.

**Spelling list:** Read the spelling words with the students. In unison, say the letter names for the tricky words "**one**" and "**by**." In "**by**," the ‹y› is taking the place of "shy ‹i›." Spellings 4-7 are color words. Other colors are covered elsewhere in the spelling lists. The longer word "color" has two syllables and can be remembered as "col" and "or" for spelling.

## Dictation

1. pain
2. deep
3. lie
4. coat
5. rescue
6. coin

1. She sleeps in a bed.
2. We sat on the train.
3. The soap fell on the ground.

## Spelling List 13

1. sad
2. let
3. **trip**
4. blue
5. orange
6. gray
7. black
8. **one**
9. **by**
10. color

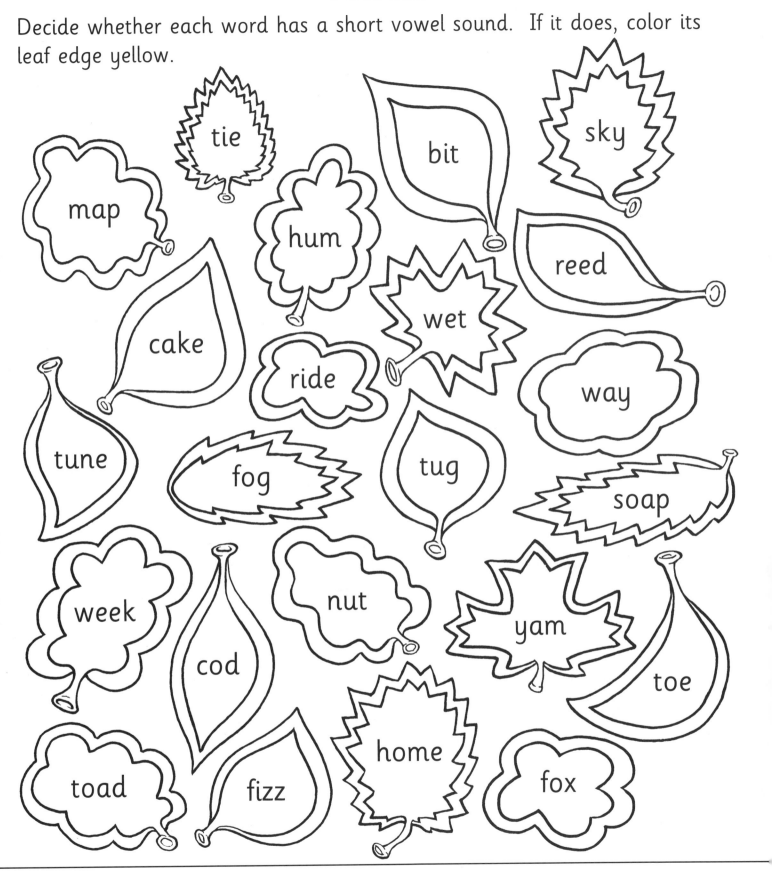

# Grammar 13 – Alphabetical order

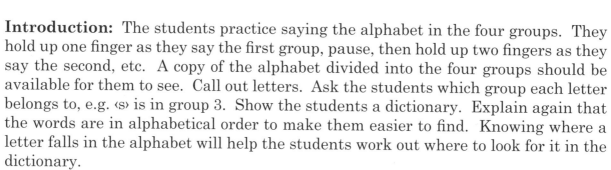

**Objective:** Develop the students' knowledge of the alphabet, and their ability to use word books and dictionaries.

**Introduction:** The students practice saying the alphabet in the four groups. They hold up one finger as they say the first group, pause, then hold up two fingers as they say the second, etc. A copy of the alphabet divided into the four groups should be available for them to see. Call out letters. Ask the students which group each letter belongs to, e.g. ‹s› is in group 3. Show the students a dictionary. Explain again that the words are in alphabetical order to make them easier to find. Knowing where a letter falls in the alphabet will help the students work out where to look for it in the dictionary.

**Main point:** Give out dictionaries for the students to look at, sharing if necessary. Call out a letter and ask the students to try finding words beginning with it in the dictionary. Repeat with other letters. This activity should be repeated often in any spare moments. Students need a lot of practice at finding the right place in the dictionary. Once they improve they can race each other to find letters.

**Grammar sheet 13:** Using a different colored pencil for each group, the students write inside the outlined capital letters. Then they write the lower-case letters next to the capitals. In the next section there are letters for the students to find in the dictionary. They find the first word for each letter and write it on the sheet. Finally the students try putting groups of letters into alphabetical order. This time the letters in each group of three are not consecutive, and are lower-case rather than capital.

**Extension activity:** Let the students look through the dictionary, reading the meaning of words that interest them. Put more letters on the board, or letter cards on the tables, for the students to find in the dictionary.

**Finishing the lesson:** Go over the sheet with the students. See which words they have found, and put the sets of letters into alphabetical order.

# Alphabetical Order

To find words in the dictionary, it helps to think of the alphabet in sections.
Use a different color for each section of the alphabet.
Write the lower-case letters next to the capital letters.

A__ B__ C__ D__ E__

F__ G__ H__ I__ J__ K__ L__ M__

N__ O__ P__ Q__ R__ S__

T__ U__ V__ W__ X__ Y__ Z__

## Using a **Dictionary**

Dictionaries tell you how a word is spelled and what it means.
Find each letter in your dictionary. Write down the first word it gives for that letter.

Aa _____   Gg _____

Ss _____   Nn _____

Oo _____   Zz _____

Put these sets of letters into alphabetical order.

| e  a  c | k  f  m | n  s  q | z  w  v |
| --- | --- | --- | --- |
| __ __ __ | __ __ __ | __ __ __ | __ __ __ |

Grammar sheet 13

# Spelling 14 – ‹a_e›

**Review:** Review some basic sounds and the other spellings covered so far. Review tricky words "said," "here," "there," "they," "go," "no," "so," "my," "one" and "by."

**Main point:** Remind the students that the main ways of writing the /ai/ sound are ‹ai›, ‹a_e› and ‹ay›. Review the ‹a_e› spelling of the /ai/ sound, which can be referred to as "‹a› hop-over ‹e›." It is important for the students to understand that the ‹e› is a "magic ‹e›." Although it makes no sound in the word, the ‹e› sends magic over the consonant before it, to change the short vowel sound to a long one. With the students, make a list of words which use ‹a_e›. Then ask them to make up sentences, using some of the words. To see the difference "magic ‹e›" makes, try covering it in some of the words and then reading them again, e.g. "cape" becomes "cap." The words could also be written onto the shape of a big bunch of grapes.

**Spelling sheet 14:** In each grape, the students write ‹a_e› in the spaces. Then they read the words and draw pictures to go with them. Afterwards they color the sheet.

**Dictation:** Read the words and sentences for the students to write down. The Dictation Master on page 171 may be reproduced onto the back of the spelling sheets for the students to write on.

**Spelling list:** Read the spelling words with the students. In unison, call out the sounds in the regular words, and say the letter names for the tricky words "only" and "old." The students can learn both of these words by saying the letter names as they write them. The longer word "baseball" has two syllables and can be remembered as "base" and "ball" for spelling.

## Dictation

1. mad
2. made
3. at
4. ate
5. scrap
6. scrape

1. Mom made a cake.
2. The gate is open.
3. She was late.

## Spelling List 14

1. ran
2. hat
3. **scar**
4. came
5. grape
6. name
7. cake
8. **only**
9. **old**
10. baseball

**Add ‹a_e› to make a word in each grape. Read the words and draw pictures for them.**

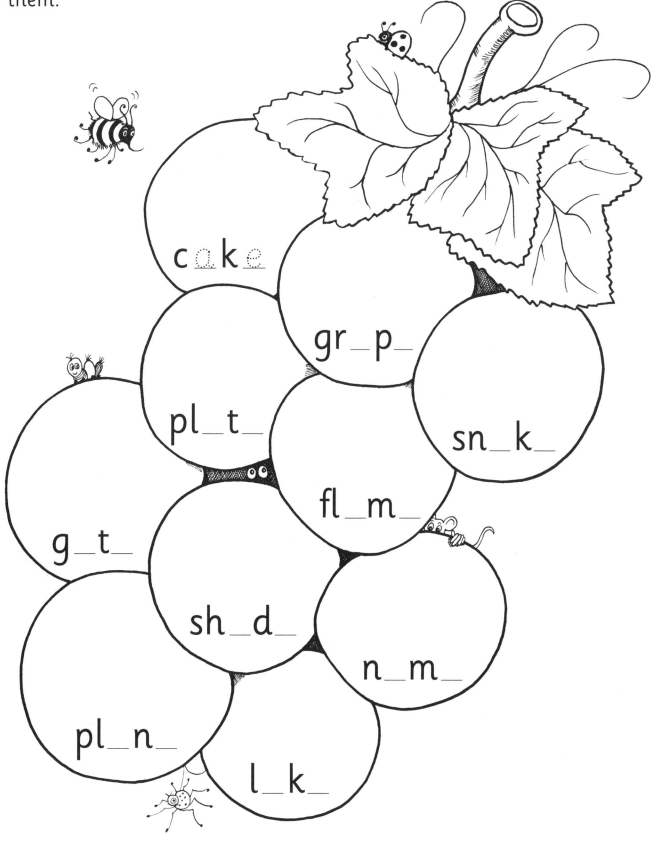

cake, gr_p_, pl_t_, sn_k_, g_t_, fl_m_, sh_d_, n_m_, pl_n_, l_k_

**Action:** Cup hand over ear and say *ai, ai, ai.*

Spelling sheet 14

# Grammar 14 – Verbs

**Objective:** Develop the students' knowledge of verbs.

**Introduction:** Review the parts of speech covered so far: proper and common nouns, and pronouns. Call out some nouns for the students to do the appropriate actions. In unison, say the pronouns with their actions. Write some sentences on the board.

Example: The bees play baseball. Billy hits the ball. He scores a run.

With the students, find the nouns and pronouns. Underline the words in the appropriate colors, using black or, if necessary, white for nouns, and pink for pronouns.

**Main point:** Tell the students that another type of word is a **verb**. For young students, a verb can be defined as a "doing" word.

Action: The action for verbs is to clench fists and move arms backwards and forwards at sides, as if running.

Color: The color for verbs is red.

Look at a picture showing lots of things happening. With the students, make a list of verbs for the actions in the picture. Usually students will say the verbs in gerund form, e.g. "clapping." Teach them that this is part of the verb "to clap." Write the infinitive "to clap" on the board. The verb root in this instance is "clap." Verb roots change according to the tense, to show when actions take place.

**Grammar sheet 14:** Help the students name the verbs for the bees' actions in the first three pictures. The students complete the infinitives by writing the verb roots, and should not add ‹ing›. Read the next three verbs with the class. The students draw a bee doing each of these actions. Finally the students think of three verbs themselves and complete the infinitives in the spaces. Then they draw a bee doing each of these actions.

**Extension activity:** Using the "Verb Bees" template on page 212, the students draw big "verb bees." They each choose one of the verbs from their sheet, and draw on the template to show their bee doing the action for it, adding legs, wings, etc. They carefully color their bees. The "verb bees" can be used to make a verb wall display.

**Finishing the lesson:** Ask the students which verbs they have written. Call out words, including proper nouns, common nouns and verbs. The students do the appropriate action for each word.

# Verbs  **Busy Bees**

Write the verb for each picture.

to _____   to _____   to _____

Draw a Bee doing each verb.

to cry   to hop   to brush

Think of 3 more verbs.

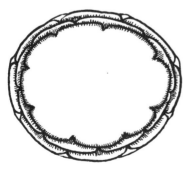 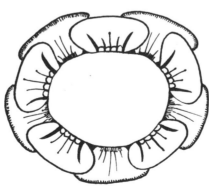 

to _____   to _____   to _____

 **Action:** Move arms backwards and forwards at sides as if running.

**Color:** Red

Grammar sheet 14

# Spelling 15 – ‹i_e›

**Review:** Review some basic sounds and the other spellings covered so far. Review tricky words "**there**," "**they**," "**go**," "**no**," "**so**," "**my**," "**one**," "**by**," "**only**" and "**old**."

**Main point:** Remind the students that the main ways of writing the /ie/ sound are ‹ie›, ‹i_e›, ‹igh› and ‹y›. Review the ‹i_e› spelling of the /ie/ sound, which can be referred to as "‹i› hop-over ‹e›." It is important for the students to understand that the ‹e› is a "magic ‹e›." Although it makes no sound in the word, the ‹e› sends magic over the consonant before it, to change the short vowel sound to a long one. With the students, make a list of words which use ‹i_e›. Then ask them to make up sentences, using some of the words. To see the difference "magic ‹e›" makes, try covering it in some of the words and then reading them again, e.g. "ride" becomes "rid." The words could also be written onto a big kite shape.

**Spelling sheet 15:** In each kite, the students write ‹i_e› in the spaces. Then they read the words and draw pictures to go with them. Afterwards they color the sheet.

**Dictation:** Read the words and sentences for the students to write down. The Dictation Master on page 171 may be reproduced onto the back of the spelling sheets for the students to write on.

**Spelling list:** Read the spelling words with the students. In unison, call out the sounds in the regular words, and say the letter names for the tricky words "**like**" and "**have**." "Like" is not really a tricky word, but the students must remember that the /ie/ sound is made with the ‹i_e› spelling. Point out to the students that "have" is only tricky because they must remember to put an ‹e› at the end. The ‹e› is there because English words do not end in ‹v›. The longer word "bridesmaid" has two syllables and can be remembered as "brides" and "maid" for spelling.

## Dictation

1. wine
2. win
3. slid
4. slide
5. spine
6. spin

1. I like my prize.
2. She has a red bike.
3. They had a kite.

## Spelling List 15

1. six
2. pad
3. **sm**ell
4. bike
5. time
6. smile
7. prize
8. **like**
9. **have**
10. bridesmaid

Add ‹i_e› to make a word in each kite. Read the words and draw pictures for them.

- kite
- f_v_
- h_v_
- b_k_
- sm_l_
- t_m_
- l_n_
- sl_d_

 **Action:** Stand to attention and salute saying *ie, ie*.

# Grammar 15 – Conjugating Verbs

**Objective:** Develop the students' knowledge of verbs.

**Introduction:** Review verbs. Call out words, including proper nouns, common nouns and verbs, for the students to do the appropriate actions. N.B. Many common verbs can also be nouns, e.g. "to smile" or "a smile." For the purposes of this lesson, try to use only those verbs which cannot also be nouns.

Examples of verbs which are rarely used as nouns:

| | | | | | |
|---|---|---|---|---|---|
| to eat | to clean | to see | to fill | to draw | to live |
| to make | to give | to hear | to sew | to wear | to bring |

Write some sentences on the board. With the students, find the proper nouns, common nouns, pronouns and verbs, and underline them in the appropriate colors.

Example:   Mom drives a car. We help Mom clean it.

**Main point:** Review pronouns and their actions (see Grammar 10). Now choose a verb, e.g. "to eat," and tell the class that they are going to join it to the pronouns. With the students, say:

"I eat,   you eat,   he eats,   she eats,   it eats,
we eat,   you eat,   they eat."

This is called **conjugating** a verb. Tell the students that for "he," "she" and "it" (the third person singular), they must add an ‹s› to the verb root. Ask the students to think of some more verbs, and conjugate them with the appropriate actions for the pronouns and verbs.

**Grammar sheet 15:** The students write inside the outlined word, Verbs, in red. Then either choose a verb together, or let each student choose a different one. The students write their verb on the line provided at the top of the sheet, and use a pink pencil to write inside the outlined pronouns. Then they write their verb beside each pronoun. Remind the students that for "he," "she" and "it," an ‹s› must be added to the verb root. Also remind them that "I," "you," "he," "she" and "it" are singular, and that "we," "you" and "they" are plural. The students draw a picture to show the person or people doing the action for their verb.

**Extension activity:** Ask the students to think of other verbs, and conjugate them.

**Finishing the lesson:** Do the action for a pronoun, and then mime a verb. See if the students can work out what you are "saying." For example, point to a girl and pretend to write something; the students answer "She writes."

# Verbs

Think of a verb and write it on the line.

to _____

Draw a picture for each person doing the verb.
Remember the 3rd person needs an ‹s› added at the end, and that for a plural you must draw more than one person.

| 1st person singular | 2nd person singular | 3rd person singular |
|---|---|---|
| | | |
| I _____ | you _____ | he she it _____ |

| 1st person plural | 2nd person plural | 3rd person plural |
|---|---|---|
| | | |
| we _____ | you _____ | they _____ |

Grammar sheet 15

# Spelling 16 – ‹o_e›

Prepare...
Flash cards:
• basic sounds
• new spellings
• tricky words
Spelling sheet 16
Spelling list 16
Tadpole shape

**Review:** Review some basic sounds and the other spellings covered so far. Review tricky words "**go**," "**no**," "**so**," "**my**," "**one**," "**by**," "**only**," "**old**," "**like**" and "**have**."

**Main point:** Remind the students that the main ways of writing the /oa/ sound are ‹oa›, ‹o_e› and ‹ow›. Review the ‹o_e› spelling of the /oa/ sound, which can be referred to as "‹o› hop-over ‹e›." It is important for the students to understand that the ‹e› is a "magic ‹e›." Although it makes no sound in the word, the ‹e› sends magic over the consonant before it, to change the short vowel sound to a long one. With the students, make a list of words which use ‹o_e›. Then ask them to make up sentences, using some of the words. To see the difference "magic ‹e›" makes, try covering it in some of the words and then reading them again, e.g. "hope" becomes "hop." The words could also be written onto a big tadpole shape.

**Spelling sheet 16:** In each tadpole, the students write ‹o_e› in the spaces. Then they read the words and draw pictures to go with them. Afterwards they color the sheet.

**Dictation:** Read the words and sentences for the students to write down. The Dictation Master on page 171 may be reproduced onto the back of the spelling sheets for the students to write on.

**Spelling list:** Read the spelling words with the students. In unison, call out the sounds in the regular words, and say the letter names for the tricky words "**live**" and "**give**." Tell the students to be particularly careful with "live," as it could take either an /ie/ sound or a short /i/ sound. When reading, they will have to work out which word is meant from the context. Again, despite the ‹i_e› spelling, "give" has an /i/ sound. The ‹e› is there because English words do not end in ‹v›. The longer word "tadpole" has two syllables and can be remembered as "tad" and "pole" for spelling.

## Dictation

1. rode
2. rod
3. hope
4. hop
5. note
6. not

1. It is time to go home.
2. Those roses are pink.
3. The mole is in his hole.

## Spelling List 16

1. cod
2. lot
3. **sn**ap
4. bone
5. nose
6. home
7. globe
8. **live**
9. **give**
10. tadpole

Add ‹**o_e**› to make a word in each tadpole. Read the words and draw pictures for them.

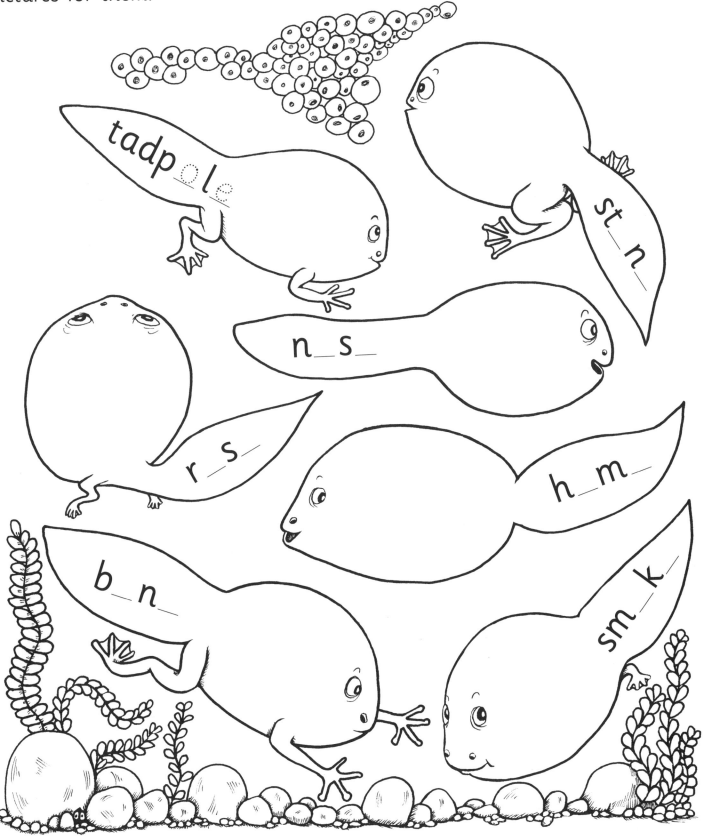

**Action:** Bring hand over mouth as if something terrible has happened and say *oh!*

Spelling sheet 16

# Grammar 16 – Past Tense

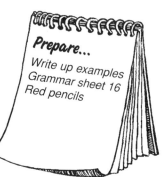

*Prepare...*
Write up examples
Grammar sheet 16
Red pencils

**Objective:** Develop the students' knowledge of the past tense. Explain that the simple past tense of a regular verb is formed by adding ‹ed› to the root.

**Introduction:** Call out words, including proper and common nouns, pronouns and verbs, for the students to do the appropriate actions. When calling out a word that can function as either a verb or a noun, e.g. "to smile" or "a smile," see which action the students do. Explain that both are right, as the word can be either a verb or a noun. The students enjoy doing both actions at once, with one hand touching their forehead while the other "runs" at the side. Ask the students how they would know whether a word was a noun or a verb, if they read it in a sentence. Write two sentences on the board, e.g. for the word "race":

Examples:   We race up the hill. (verb)    We run in a race. (noun)

With the students, look at the words in the sentences. Decide which parts of speech they are, and underline them in the appropriate colors. It is important that the students realize that a word can function as more than one part of speech, and that they need to look at the context to see how it is being used.

**Main point:** Explain that verbs often change to show when the action takes place. So far the verbs taught have all been in the **present tense**, which means they describe actions taking place now. If, however, the verb describes an action which has already taken place, it should be in the **past tense**. So "Today I wish" is in the present and "Yesterday I wished" is in the past. The past tense of a regular verb is made by adding the suffix ‹ed› to the root. If the root ends with an ‹e›, the students should remove it before adding ‹ed›. The ‹ed› can make three different sounds, either /id/ as in "hated," /d/ as in "saved," or /t/ as in "missed."

Actions:    The action for the present tense is pointing towards the floor with the palm of the hand.
The action for the past tense is pointing backwards over the shoulder with a thumb.

Color:    The color for verbs is red.

Call out verbs in the present and past tenses, for the students to do the actions.

**Grammar sheet 16:** With the students, read through the sheet. The students write the verbs in the past tense. Then they decide if the sentences are in the present or past tenses.

**Extension activity:** Put some sentences on the board in the present tense and ask the students to write the sentences in the past tense. The Writing Master on page 172 may be reproduced onto the back of the grammar sheets for them to write on.

**Finishing the lesson:** With the students, go through the sheet and any extra work.

# Past Tense

Verbs  Red

The simplest way to make the past tense is by adding ‹ed› to the verb.

| **Today I talk** | talk + ed | **Yesterday I talked** |

If a verb already ends with an ‹e›, cross it off and then add ‹ed›.

| **Today I smile** | smil~~e~~ + ed | **Yesterday I smiled** |

Put these words into the past tense.

| Present | Past | Present | Past |
|---|---|---|---|
| jump | _____ | hope | _____ |
| paint | _____ | play | _____ |
| like | _____ | wave | _____ |
| shout | _____ | skate | _____ |

Underline the verbs in red.
Then decide if these sentences are in the present or past.

| | |
|---|---|
| She brushed her hair. | (past) / present |
| They look out of the window. | past / present |
| I cooked lunch. | past / present |
| The race started in the park. | past / present |

 **Action (Past):** Point thumb backwards over shoulder.

Grammar sheet 16

# Spelling 17 – ‹u_e›

**Review:** Review some basic sounds and the other spellings covered so far. Review tricky words "**so**," "**my**," "**one**," "**by**," "**only**," "**old**," "**like**," "**have**," "**live**" and "**give**."

**Main point:** Remind the students that the main ways of writing the /ue/ sound are ‹ue›, ‹u_e› and ‹ew›. However, ‹u_e› is a difficult spelling because it often makes an /oo/ sound, as in "rude." Review the ‹u_e› spelling of the /ue/ and /oo/ sounds, which can be referred to as "‹u› hop-over ‹e›." It is important for the students to understand that the ‹e› is a "magic ‹e›." Although it makes no sound in the word, the ‹e› sends magic over the consonant before it, to change the short vowel sound to a long one. With the students, make a list of words which use ‹u_e›. Then ask them to make up sentences, using some of the words. To see the difference "magic ‹e›" makes, try covering it in some of the words and then reading them again, e.g. "use" becomes "us." The words could also be written onto a big "tune" note shape.

**Spelling sheet 17:** In each note of the tune, the students write ‹u_e› in the spaces. Then they read the words and draw pictures to go with them. Afterwards they color the sheet.

**Dictation:** Read the words and sentences for the students to write down. The Dictation Master on page 171 may be reproduced onto the back of the spelling sheets for the students to write on.

**Spelling list:** Read the spelling words with the students. In unison, call out the sounds in the regular words, and say the letter names for the tricky words "**little**" and "**down**." The longer word "useless" has two syllables and can be remembered as "use" and "less" for spelling.

## Dictation

1. us
2. use
3. cub
4. cube
5. tube
6. tub

1. They broke a rule.
2. Soon we will see the duke.
3. The girl played a tune.

## Spelling List 17

1. bus
2. pot
3. **sw**im
4. cube
5. tune
6. used
7. excuse
8. **little**
9. **down**
10. useless

**Add ‹u_e› to make a word in each note of the tune. Read the words and draw pictures for them.**

cube, m_l_, t_b_, t_n_, d_k_

**Action:** Move head forward as if it is the cuckoo, saying *oo*. (This comes from the action for *u oo*.)

**Action:** Point to people around you and say *you, you.*

Spelling sheet 17

# Grammar 17 – Doubling Rule

*Prepare...*
*Grammar sheet 17*
*Red pencils*

**Objective:** Develop the students' ability to recognize the short vowels in words, so that they learn when to apply the doubling rule before adding ‹ed›.

**Introduction:** With the students, say the alphabet in the four groups. See if the students can do this without reading it. Review the vowels. Review present and past tenses. Call out verbs in the present and past tenses for the students to do the actions (see Grammar 16).

**Main point:** Tell the students that endings which are added to words are called **suffixes**. If a word has a short vowel sound, it is important to be careful when adding a suffix that starts with a vowel, such as ‹ed›. This is because the ‹e› behaves like a "magic ‹e›", and changes the vowel sound in the word. For example, if ‹ed› is added to "hop" it becomes "hoped." The short /o/ sound becomes a long /oa/, which completely changes the meaning of the word. To avoid this we use the **doubling rule**. The consonant at the end of the verb root is doubled to make a "wall." The "magic" from the ‹e› cannot jump over a wall of more than one letter. (See picture on page 18.) The students are unlikely to remember this rule immediately, but will gradually do so through revisiting and applying it.

Examples of verb roots needing the doubling rule:

    grab      beg      fit      stop      hum

If the students ask about a word like "stamped," explain that it already has a wall made by the two consonants ‹m› and ‹p›. Words that do not have short vowel sounds, e.g. "look," "play" and "bark," do not need a wall, and so do not need to double the last consonant.

**Grammar sheet 17:** The students write the verb roots in the past tense, remembering to apply the doubling rule.

**Extension activity:** Ask the students to draw a picture of the "magic" from the ‹e› being unable to cross a thick "wall" of two consonants.

**Finishing the lesson:** Call out some verbs. The students listen for the vowel sounds. For verbs which have a short vowel sound, they do the actions for Inky and the box (see picture on page 17). For verbs that do not, the students put their hands in their laps.

# Past Tense

Write these verbs in the simple past tense.

Grammar sheet 17

# Spelling 18 – ‹wh›

**Review:** Review some basic sounds and the other spellings covered so far. Review tricky words "**one**," "**by**," "**only**," "**old**," "**like**," "**have**," "**live**," "**give**," "**little**" and "**down**."

**Main point:** Review the ‹wh› spelling of the /w/ sound. With the students, make a list of words which use it, or give them some examples. Then ask them to make up sentences, using some of the words. The words could also be written onto a big whale shape.

**Spelling sheet 18:** The students write inside the outlined wh. Then in each whale they write a ‹wh› word and draw a picture for that word. Afterwards they color the sheet.

**Dictation:** Read the words and sentences for the students to write down. The Dictation Master on page 171 may be reproduced onto the back of the spelling sheets for the students to write on.

**Spelling list:** Read the spelling words with the students. In unison, call out the sounds in the regular words, and say the letter names for the tricky words "**what**" and "**when**." Tell the students that the question words "what," "where," "when," "why," "who" and "which" are all ‹wh› words. Other question words will be covered in later spelling lists. The longer word "whenever" has three syllables. It can be remembered as the two shorter words "when" and "ever" for spelling.

## Dictation

1. when
2. whisk
3. whizz
4. which
5. whale
6. whisker

1. My cat is black and white.
2. The rabbit has long whiskers.
3. What did you whisper?

## Spelling List 18

1. did
2. cut
3. **tw**in
4. whale
5. wheel
6. white
7. whisper
8. **what**
9. **when**
10. whenever

**Write a ‹wh› word and draw a picture in each whale.**

 **Action:** Blow onto open hand, as if you are the wind, and say *wh, wh, wh.*

Spelling sheet 18

# Grammar 18 – The Future

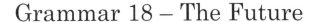

**Objective:** Develop the students' understanding of verbs, so they know that a verb can describe the past, present or future.

**Introduction:** Review present and past tenses with the students. Call out verbs in the present and past tenses for the students to do the appropriate actions (see Grammar 16). Call out some verbs in the present tense. Make a point of choosing verbs which have a regular simple past tense, such as "to cook," "to hop" or "to race." Ask the students to put these verbs into the past. Then call out some verbs in the past tense and ask the students to put them into the present.

**Main point:** When a verb describes an action taking place in the future, the verb root does not take a suffix, as in the past tense. Instead it has an extra word put in front of it. The extra word is another verb, called an auxiliary verb. The auxiliary verb used to describe the future is the verb "to be." "Shall" is added for the first person ("I" and "we"), and "will" for the second and third persons. (The verb "to be" is completely irregular, but is essential. The future of the verb "to be" is "I shall, you will, he/she/it will, we shall, you will, they will.")

Example of a verb in the future: "to jump":

"I shall jump, you will jump, he will jump, she will jump,
it will jump, we shall jump, you will jump, they will jump."

Actions:   The action for verbs which describe the future is pointing to the front.

Color:     The color for verbs is red.

Call out some verbs and ask the students to put them into the future.

**Grammar sheet 18:** The students write the verbs in the past tense in the "Yesterday" column, and in the future in the "Tomorrow" column. Then they write some sentences about what they did yesterday and what they will do tomorrow.

**Extension activity:** Ask the students to write some more sentences about what they did yesterday. The Writing Master on page 172 may be reproduced onto the back of the grammar sheets for the students to write on.

**Finishing the lesson:** With the students, choose a verb and conjugate it in the past, present and future.

# Future

|  Past<br>Yesterday |  | Future<br>Tomorrow |
|---|---|---|
| I _____ | I cook | I ____ _____ |
| I _____ | I listen | I ____ _____ |
| I _____ | I skate | I ____ _____ |
| I _____ | I walk | I ____ _____ |

Write some sentences about what you did yesterday.

_____

_____

_____

Write some sentences about what you will do tomorrow.

_____

_____

_____

A sentence must have a verb.  Underline the verbs in your sentences in red.

 **Action (Future):** Point to the front.

Grammar sheet 18

# Spelling 19 – ‹ay›

**Review:** Review some basic sounds and the other spellings covered so far. Review tricky words "**only**," "**old**," "**like**," "**have**," "**live**," "**give**," "**little**," "**down**," "**what**" and "**when**."

**Main point:** Remind the students that the main ways of writing the /ai/ sound are ‹ai›, ‹a_e› and ‹ay›. Review the ‹ay› spelling of the /ai/ sound. Tell the students that the ‹ay› spelling is often used at the end of words. The ‹y› takes the place of "shy ‹i›," since the letter ‹i› does not like to be at the end of words. Then ask the children to make up sentences, using some of the words. The words could also be written onto a big crayon shape.

**Spelling sheet 19:** The students write inside the outlined ay. Then in each crayon they write an ‹ay› word and draw a picture for that word. Afterwards they color the sheet.

**Dictation:** Read the words and sentences for the students to write down. The Dictation Master on page 171 may be reproduced onto the back of the spelling sheets for the students to write on.

**Spelling list:** Read the spelling words with the students. In unison, call out the sounds in the regular words, and say the letter names for the tricky words "**why**" and "**where**." Tell the students that the question words "what," "when," "why," "who," "where" and "which" are all ‹wh› words (see Spelling 18, pages 94-5). The longer word "playground" has two syllables, and can be remembered as "play" and "ground" for spelling.

### Dictation

1. hay
2. way
3. play
4. tray
5. clay
6. Sunday

1. You can all stay here.
2. Today is hot.
3. I made this from clay.

### Spelling List 19

1. an
2. cat
3. **skin**
4. say
5. away
6. play
7. today
8. **why**
9. **where**
10. playground

Write an ‹**ay**› word and draw a picture in each crayon.

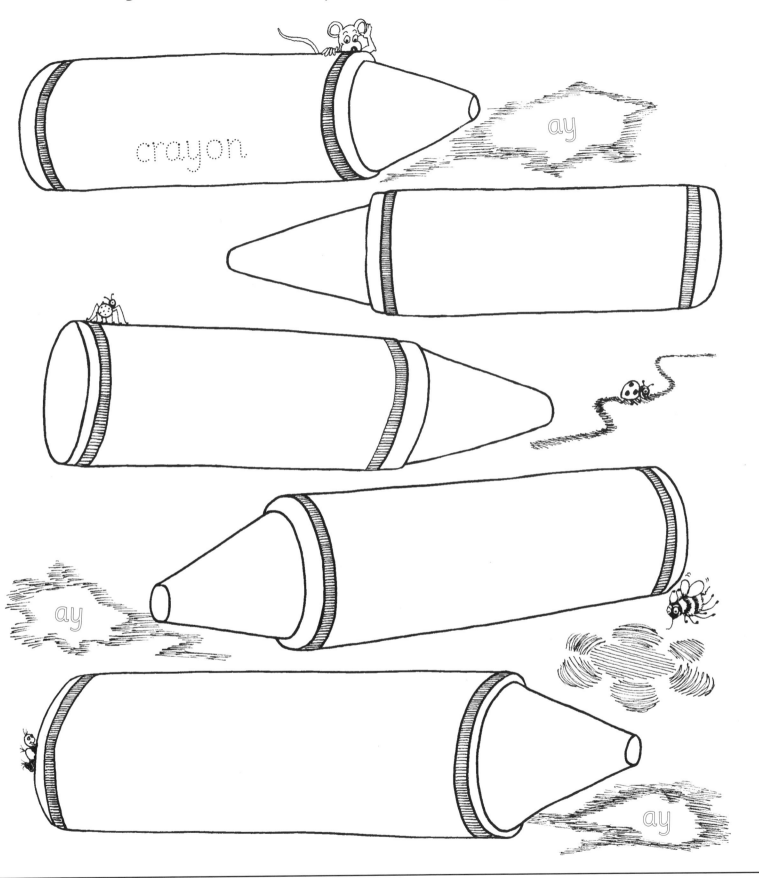

**Action:** Cup hand over ear and say *ai, ai, ai.*

Spelling sheet 19

# Grammar 19 – Alphabetical order

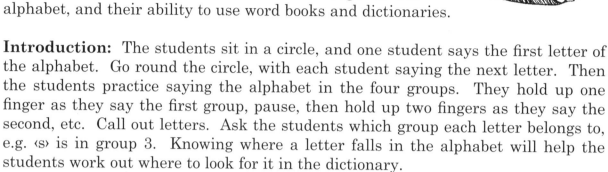

**Prepare...**
Alphabet in four groups
Write up examples
Grammar sheet 19
Colored pencils
Dictionaries

**Objective:** Develop the students' knowledge of the alphabet, and their ability to use word books and dictionaries.

**Introduction:** The students sit in a circle, and one student says the first letter of the alphabet. Go round the circle, with each student saying the next letter. Then the students practice saying the alphabet in the four groups. They hold up one finger as they say the first group, pause, then hold up two fingers as they say the second, etc. Call out letters. Ask the students which group each letter belongs to, e.g. ‹s› is in group 3. Knowing where a letter falls in the alphabet will help the students work out where to look for it in the dictionary.

**Main point:** Look at a copy of the dictionary. Explain that the words are listed in alphabetical order, to make them easier to find. Words can be arranged in alphabetical order just as letters can. Write some words on the board. To avoid confusion at this stage, make sure each word begins with a different letter. The students look at the first letter of each word, to help them arrange the words in alphabetical order.

**Grammar sheet 19:** Using a different colored pencil for each group, the students write inside the outlined lower-case letters. Then they write the capitals next to the lower-case letters. In the next section the students put groups of letters into alphabetical order. Then they try putting groups of words into alphabetical order.

**Extension activity:** Give out dictionaries for the students to look at, sharing if necessary. Write some letters on the board. Ask the students to find words beginning with these letters in the dictionary. The Writing Master on page 172 may be reproduced onto the back of the grammar sheets for the students to write on. If the students are able, they could also copy out the words' meanings.

**Finishing the lesson:** Go over the sheet, with the students putting the words into alphabetical order. Call out letters and see if the students can find the right section for them in the dictionary.

# Alphabetical Order

Use a different color for each section of the alphabet.
Write the capital letters next to the lower-case letters.

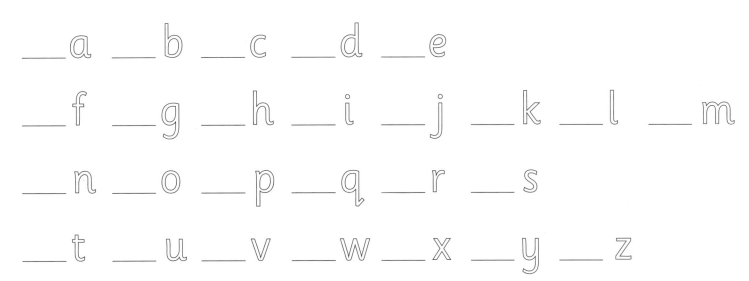

Put these sets of letters into alphabetical order.

| F  B  X  O | T  C  N  H | q  w  i  r |
|---|---|---|
| __ __ __ __ | __ __ __ __ | __ __ __ __ |

Put these words into alphabetical order.

Inky    Snake    Bee

_____  _____  _____

pear    apple    orange

_____  _____  _____

Grammar sheet 19

# Spelling 20 – ‹ea›

**Review:** Review some basic sounds and the other spellings covered so far. Review tricky words "**like**," "**have**," "**live**," "**give**," "**little**," "**down**," "**what**," "**when**," "**why**" and "**where**."

**Main point:** Remind the students that the main ways of writing the /ee/ sound are ‹ee› and ‹ea›. Review the ‹ea› spelling of the /ee/ sound. With the students, make a list of words which use it. Then ask them to make up sentences, using some of the words. The words could also be written onto a big teapot shape.

**Spelling sheet 20:** The students write inside the outlined ea. Then in each teapot they write an ‹ea› word and draw a picture for that word. Afterwards they color the sheet.

**Dictation:** Read the words and sentences for the students to write down. The Dictation Master on page 171 may be reproduced onto the back of the spelling sheets for the students to write on.

**Spelling list:** Read the spelling words with the students. In unison, call out the sounds in the regular words, and say the letter names for the tricky words "**who**" and "**which**." Tell the students that the question words "what," "where," "when," "why," "who" and "which" are all ‹wh› words (see Spelling 18, pages 94-5). The longer word "seashell" has two syllables and can be remembered as "sea" and "shell" for spelling.

## Dictation

1. sea
2. peas
3. meat
4. clean
5. leaf
6. teapot

1. My room is neat and clean.
2. She took the dog to the beach.
3. He has peas in his garden.

## Spelling List 20

1. met
2. web
3. **sp**in
4. tea
5. heat
6. leaf
7. each
8. **who**
9. **which**
10. seashell

**Write an ‹ea› word and draw a picture in each teapot.**

 **Action:** Put hands on head as if ears on a donkey and say *ee*. (This comes from the *ee or* action.)

# Grammar 20 – Nouns

**Objective:** Develop the students' understanding of nouns, and their ability to identify nouns in sentences.

**Introduction:** Revise the parts of speech covered so far: proper and common nouns, pronouns and verbs. Call out words for the students to do the appropriate actions. Remember that some words can function as both nouns and verbs, so the students can do both actions.

**Main point:** Look at the picture on Grammar sheet 20. Ask the students to give examples of nouns. Remind them that we can put "a" (the indefinite article) or "the" (the definite article) before those that are common nouns. Write some sentences on the board. Go through the sentences, finding the proper and common nouns with the students.

Examples:  The farmer drives a tractor.
My dog goes to the vet on Monday.

Underline the nouns in black. If using a blackboard, explain that as there is no black chalk, white chalk is used instead.

**Grammar sheet 20:** The students look at the picture and write six nouns for things they can see. Remind them about when to use the indefinite articles "a" and "an" (see Grammar 8). Then the students read the sentences underneath and underline the nouns in black. Explain that there can be more than one noun in a sentence.

**Extension activity:** The students write some sentences about the picture and underline the nouns. The Writing Master on page 172 may be reproduced onto the back of the grammar sheets for the students to write on. The students could also look up their six nouns in the dictionary.

**Finishing the lesson:** Go over the sheet, with the students identifying the nouns.

# Nouns

Write 6 nouns for what you can see in the picture.

a _____    the _____

a _____    the _____

a _____    the _____

Underline the nouns in these sentences in black.
There can be more than one noun in a sentence.

1. The cat is black and white.

2. Kate drives a red tractor.

3. The sheep are on the hills.

4. On Andrew's farm, there are cows, horses, sheep, pigs and chickens.

Grammar sheet 20

# Spelling 21 – ‹igh›

**Review:** Review some basic sounds and the other spellings covered so far. Review tricky words "**live**," "**give**," "**little**," "**down**," "**what**," "**when**," "**why**," "**where**," "**who**" and "**which**."

**Main point:** Remind the students that the main ways of writing the /ie/ sound are ‹ie›, ‹i_e›, ‹igh› and ‹y›. Review the ‹igh› spelling of the /ie/ sound. With the students, make a list of words which use it. Then ask them to make up sentences, using some of the words. The words could also be written onto a big light-bulb shape.

**Spelling sheet 21:** The students write inside the outlined igh. Then in each light bulb they write an ‹igh› word and draw a picture for that word. Afterwards they color the sheet.

**Dictation:** Read the words and sentences for the students to write down. The Dictation Master on page 171 may be reproduced onto the back of the spelling sheets for the students to write on.

**Spelling list:** Read the spelling words with the students. In unison, call out the sounds in the regular words, and say the letter names for the tricky words "**any**" and "**many**." The longer word "frightening" has three syllables and can be remembered as "frigh," "ten" and "ing," for spelling  It helps the students remember the spelling if they emphasize the /e/ sound in the second syllable, pronouncing it to rhyme with "pen."

| Dictation | Spelling List 21 |
|---|---|
| 1. high  4. sight | 1. lip |
| 2. sigh  5. bright | 2. his |
| 3. thigh  6. flight | 3. went |
|  | 4. night |
|  | 5. high |
| 1. It was a dark night. | 6. might |
| 2. My dad had a fright. | 7. light |
| 3. There was a bright light. | 8. **any** |
|  | 9. **many** |
|  | 10. frightening |

Write an ‹**igh**› word and draw a picture in each light bulb.

**Action:** Stand to attention and salute saying *ie, ie*.

Spelling sheet 21

# Grammar 21 – Adjectives

**Objective:** Develop the students' understanding of adjectives. Adjectives are words which describe nouns.

**Introduction:** Ask each student for an example of a common noun, e.g. "a dog," "a hat."

**Main point:** Find, or draw, a picture of some snakes. If the snakes are drawn, color them in. Ask the students what the picture shows, and which part of speech the word "snake" is (i.e. a noun). Write the following sentence on the board:

Sentence: This is a snake.

Underline the noun. Tell the students that this sentence does not tell us very much about the snake. Choose one of the snakes in the picture. Ask the students for words to describe the snake, which could be added to the sentence to make it more interesting, e.g. "long," "green," "spotty," "sad," "old." Choose one of the describing words and add it to the sentence on the board. Tell the students that a word which describes a noun is called an **adjective**.

Action: The action for an adjective is to touch the side of the temple with a fist.

Color: The color for adjectives is blue.

Underline the adjective in the sentence in blue, while the students do the action. Choose some more snakes from the picture and ask for adjectives to describe them. Choose one of the snakes and, with the students, find as many adjectives to describe it as possible.

**Grammar sheet 21:** The students read the adjectives in the speech bubbles. Then they color each snake to make it fit its adjective. The "long" snake needs to have its "long" body added. The students complete the phrase at the bottom of the sheet by writing three more adjectives which might describe a snake. Then they color the snake underneath to fit these adjectives.

**Extension activity:** The reproducible master on page 215 shows a section of a snake's body. The students each choose an adjective and color their section of the snake accordingly. The sections can then be stuck together, with a head and tail added (see pages 214 and 216), to make "Adjective Snakes." The snakes can have any number of middle sections. The finished snake can be used for display.

**Finishing the lesson:** With the students, look at any finished "adjective snakes" and say the phrase "a _____ , _____ , _____ snake," filling in the blanks with appropriate adjectives.

# Adjectives  Blue

Color the snakes to make them fit the adjectives.

You can use more than one adjective at a time.
Color this snake to make it fit your description.

a _____ , _____ , _____ snake

 **Action:** Touch side of temple with fist.

Grammar sheet 21

# Spelling 22 – ⟨y⟩

**Review:** Review some basic sounds and the other spellings covered so far. Review tricky words "**little**," "**down**," "**what**," "**when**," "**why**," "**where**," "**who**," "**which**," "**any**" and "**many**."

**Main point:** Remind the students that the main ways of writing the /ie/ sound are ⟨ie⟩, ⟨i_e⟩, ⟨igh⟩ and ⟨y⟩. Review the ⟨y⟩ spelling of the /ie/ sound. With the students, make a list of words which use it. Then ask them to make up sentences, using some of the words. The words could also be written onto a big frying-pan shape.

**Spelling sheet 22:** The students write inside the outlined y. Then in each frying pan they write a ⟨y⟩ word and draw a picture for that word. Afterwards they color the sheet.

**Dictation:** Read the words and sentences for the students to write down. The Dictation Master on page 171 may be reproduced onto the back of the spelling sheets for the students to write on.

**Spelling list:** Read the spelling words with the students. In unison, call out the sounds in the regular words, and say the letter names for the tricky words "**more**" and "**before**." The longer word "myself" has two syllables and can be remembered as "my" and "self" for spelling.

## Dictation

1. my
2. dry
3. pry
4. crying
5. flying
6. trying

1. Pigs live in a sty.
2. They are flying with me.
3. He was trying to sing the song.

## Spelling List 22

1. win
2. sit
3. **stop**
4. fry
5. dry
6. crying
7. sky
8. **more**
9. **before**
10. myself

Write a ‹y› word and draw a picture in each frying pan.

 **Action:** Stand to attention and salute saying *ie, ie*.

Spelling sheet 22

# Grammar 22 – Adjectives

**Objective:** Develop the students' ability to identify nouns and adjectives in sentences.

**Introduction:** Review common nouns. Choose a noun, e.g. "a horse." Ask one student to say the noun with an adjective to describe it, e.g. "a big horse." Ask each student in turn to repeat what has been said and to add a new adjective, as in a memory game, e.g. "a big, brown horse," "a big, brown, kind horse," etc.

**Main point:** Review adjectives. Think of some nouns, e.g. "chair," "sweater," "dog," "sandwich." Ask the students for an adjective to go with each noun. Use one of their suggestions to make a simple sentence, and write it on the board, e.g. "He had a little dog." Underline the noun in black and the adjective in blue.

**Grammar sheet 22:** The students read the adjectives in the snake. Then they read the sentences in the middle of the sheet. They choose one of the adjectives for each sentence, and write it in the space. The adjectives can be used more than once.

**Extension activity:** The students underline the nouns in black and the adjectives in blue.

**Finishing the lesson:** Go over the sheet with the students, seeing which adjectives they have chosen for each sentence. As long as their adjectives make sense in the sentences, the students' answers are right.

# Adjectives

Find an adjective to describe each noun. There are some adjectives in the snake to help you. Underline the nouns in black.

A _____ snake hisses.

My _____ shirt is new.

The _____ dog barks.

Her _____ car stopped.

The sky is _____.

The tree is _____.

The _____ flowers smell.

The movie was _____.

His _____ balloon burst.

My _____ coat is warm.

*Adjectives on snake:* red, striped, green, long, yellow, pretty, blue, tall, pink, small, spotty

# Spelling 23 – ‹ow›

**Review:** Review some basic sounds and the other spellings covered so far. Review tricky words "**what**," "**when**," "**why**," "**where**," "**who**," "**which**," "**any**," "**many**," "**more**" and "**before**."

**Main point:** Remind the students that the main ways of writing the /oa/ sound are ‹oa›, ‹o_e› and ‹ow›. Review the ‹ow› spelling of the /oa/ sound. With the students, make a list of words which use it. Then ask them to make up sentences, using some of the words. The words could also be written onto a big snowman shape.

**Spelling sheet 23:** The students write inside the outlined ow. Then in each snowman they write an ‹ow› word, and draw a picture for that word. Afterwards they color the sheet.

**Dictation:** Read the words and sentences for the students to write down. The Dictation Master on page 171 may be reproduced onto the back of the spelling sheets for the students to write on.

**Spelling list:** Read the spelling words with the students. In unison, call out the sounds in the regular words, and say the letter names for the tricky words "**other**" and "**were**." For "other," the students should use the "Say it as it sounds" method, pronouncing the ‹o› in the first syllable to rhyme with "bother." For "were," the students should say the names of the letters as they write them. The longer word "snowman" has two syllables and can be remembered as "snow" and "man" for spelling.

## Dictation

1. own
2. low
3. mow
4. show
5. grow
6. throw

1. It has started snowing.
2. The seeds have grown well.
3. There is a show on Monday.

## Spelling List 23

1. box
2. job
3. bu**lb**
4. own
5. grow
6. elbow
7. yellow
8. **other**
9. **were**
10. snowman

Write an ‹**ow**› word and draw a picture in each snowman.

snow

**Action:** Bring hand over mouth as if something terrible has happened and say *oh!*

Spelling sheet 23

# Grammar 23 – Final Blends

**Objective:** Develop the students' ability to recognize final blends.

**Introduction:** Review initial blends. Hold up flash cards of initial blends for the students to read. Then call out blends for the students to say which letters are in them.

**Main point:** Tell the students that not all blends come at the beginning of words. Some come at the end of words and are called final blends. Hold up some flash cards of final blends and ask the students to blend them. On the board, write an example of a word using each blend. Call out some of the final blends and ask the students which letter sounds are in them.

Examples:    lamp      tent      sink      pond      tusk
             bank      felt      milk      frost     bump
             hand      vest      wind      cold      dust

**Grammar sheet 23:** The students read the outlined final blends and write inside them. Then they read the unfinished words and try adding the final blends to each of them. They try each final blend in turn until they find one which completes the word, e.g. ‹be› and ‹mp› makes "bemp," which is not a real word, whereas ‹be› and ‹lt› makes "belt," which is. Once they have found a blend to complete a word, the students write it in and draw a picture for the word. As long as the students have made real words, their answers are right, so ‹sta› could become either "stamp" or "stand."

**Extension activity:** Write the unfinished words and final blends out on cards. Give the cards out to the students. They see how many other words they can make. The Writing Master on page 172 may be reproduced onto the back of the grammar sheets for them to write on. This exercise could be repeated with different unfinished words and final blends.

**Finishing the lesson:** Go over the sheet with the students, seeing which words they have made.

# Final Blends

Try the different final blends until you find one that makes a word. Write the blends in and draw pictures for the words you have made.

| mp | lt | nt |
|----|----|----|
| st | nd | ft |

sta_____  so_____  be_____

a_____  ne_____  ha_____

la_____  mi_____  te_____

Grammar sheet 23

# Spelling 24 – ‹ew›

**Review:** Review some basic sounds and the other spellings covered so far. In unison tricky words "why," "where," "who," "which," "any," "many," "more," "before," "other" and "were."

**Main point:** Remind the students that the main ways of writing the /ue/ sound are ‹ue›, ‹u_e› and ‹ew›. However, ‹ew› is a difficult spelling because it often makes an /oo/ sound, as in "grew." Teach the ‹ew› spelling of the /ue/ and /oo/ sounds. With the students, make a list of words which use it. Then ask them to make up sentences, using some of the words. The words could also be written onto a big jewel shape.

**Spelling sheet 24:** The students write inside the outlined ew. Then in each jewel they write an ‹ew› word and draw a picture for that word. Afterwards they color the sheet.

**Dictation:** Read the words and sentences for the students to write down. The Dictation Master on page 171 may be reproduced onto the back of the spelling sheets for the students to write on.

**Spelling list:** Read the spelling words with the students. In unison, call out the sounds in the regular words, and say the letter names for the tricky words "**because**" and "**want**." For "because," tell the students to use the mnemonic "**b**ig **e**lephants **c**atch **a**nts **u**nder **s**mall **e**lephants." For "want" the students should use the "Say it as it sounds" method, pronouncing it to rhyme with "ant." The longer word "newspaper" has three syllables and can be remembered as "news," "pa" and "per," for spelling.

## Dictation

1. few
2. new
3. pew
4. grew
5. chew
6. drew

1. A few more can go.
2. There is my new bike.
3. He drew a newt.

## Spelling List 24

1. bud
2. sun
3. hel**d**
4. few
5. flew
6. grew
7. chew
8. **because**
9. **want**
10. newspaper

Write an ‹**ew**› word and draw a picture in each jewel.

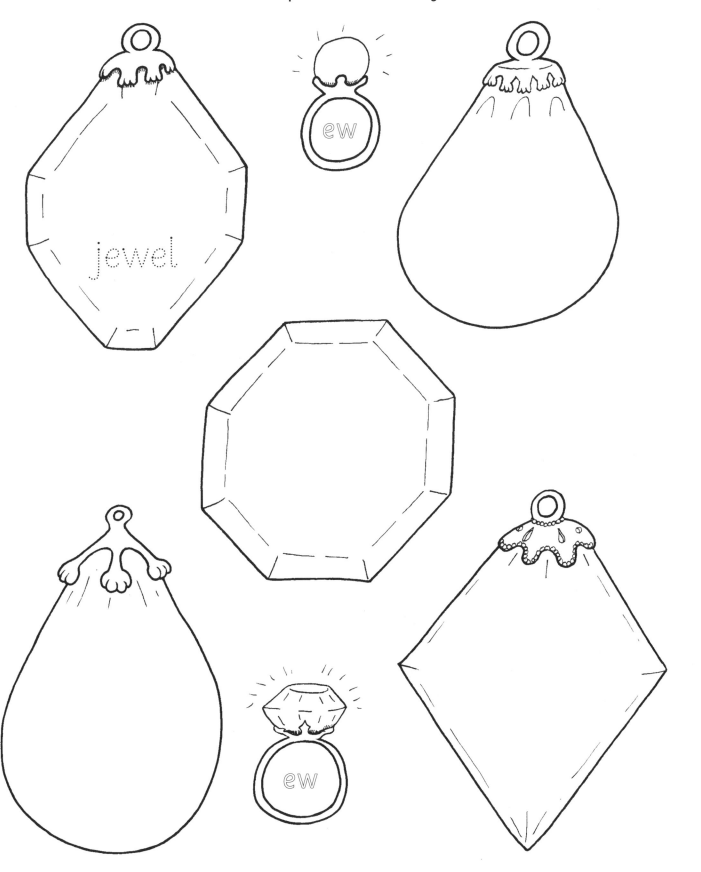

 **Action:** Move head forward as if it is the cuckoo, saying *oo*. (This comes from the action for *u oo*.)

 **Action:** Point to people around you and say *you, you*.

Spelling sheet 24

# Grammar 24 – Compound Words

**Objective:** Develop the students' ability to recognize compound words.

**Introduction:** Review initial and final blends. Hold up flash cards of the blends for the students to read. Then call out blends for the students to name the letters in them.

**Main point:** Compound words are words made of two (or more) shorter words joined together. Draw some "picture word sums" on the board for the students to work out the compound words.

Example:     picture of star  +  picture of fish  =  "starfish"

Other words which could be used:

|  |  |  |
|---|---|---|
| blue + bell | fire + fly | foot + ball |
| tooth + brush | black + bird | cow + boy/girl |
| sun + flower | arm + chair | ear + ring |
| rain + coat | sea + shell | butter + fly |

**Grammar sheet 24:** The students read the words in the birds' wings and tails. Then they try adding the "tail words" to the "wing words" to make compound words. They try each "tail word" in turn until they find one that makes sense, e.g. "mail" and "ball" makes "mailball" which is not a real word, whereas "mail" and "man" makes "mailman."

**Extension activity:** Give the students some more words, on the board or on cards, and see how many compound words they can make using them. The "Compound Birds" sheet on page 218 may be reproduced and cut up to make sets of compound word puzzles.

| Examples: | rain + bow | shoe + lace | lunch + time |
|---|---|---|---|
|  | lunch + box | home + work | home + time |
|  | shoe + box | mail + box | fire + work |

**Finishing the lesson:** Go over the sheet with the students, checking the compound words they have made.

# Compound Words

The compound birds have muddled up their tails. Can you sort them out?

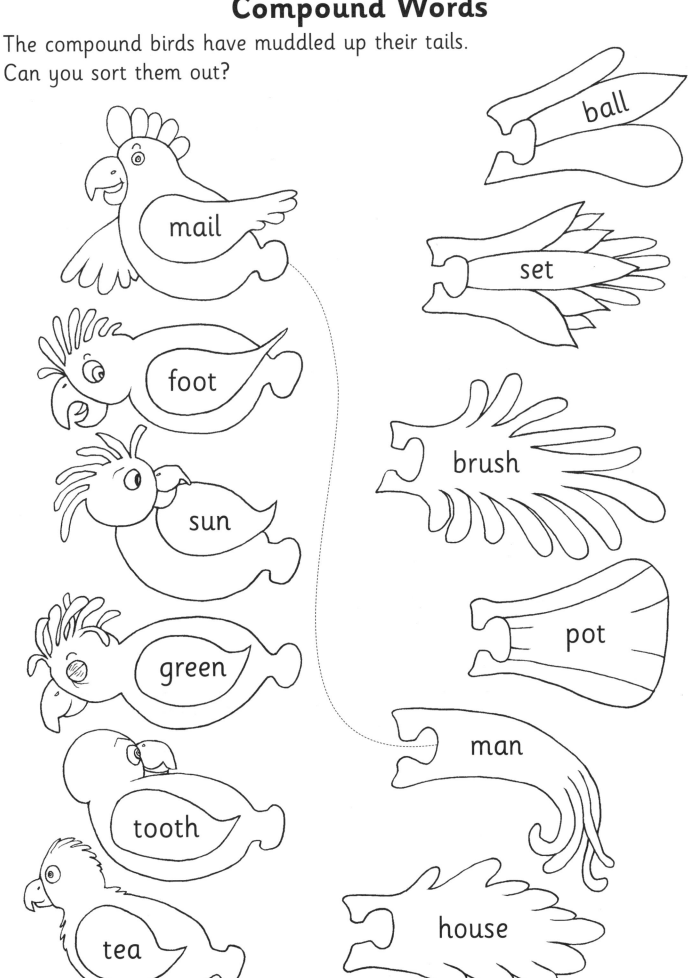

Grammar sheet 24

# Spelling 25 – ‹ou›

**Review:** Review some basic sounds and the other spellings covered so far. Review tricky words "**who**," "**which**," "**any**," "**many**," "**more**," "**before**," "**other**," "**were**," "**because**" and "**want**."

**Main point:** Remind the students that the main ways of writing the /ou/ sound are ‹ou› and ‹ow›. Review the ‹ou› spelling of the /ou/ sound. With the students, make a list of words which use it. Then ask them to make up sentences, using some of the words. The words could also be written onto a big house shape.

**Spelling sheet 25:** The students write inside the outlined ou. Then in each house they write an ‹ou› word and draw a picture for that word. Afterwards they color the sheet.

**Dictation:** Read the words and sentences for the students to write down. The Dictation Master on page 171 may be reproduced onto the back of the spelling sheets for the students to write on.

**Spelling list:** Read the spelling words with the students. In unison, call out the sounds in the regular words, and say the letter names for the tricky words "**saw**" and "**put**." The longer word "outside" is a compound word. It has two syllables and can be remembered as "out" and "side" for spelling.

### Dictation

1. our
2. loud
3. south
4. flour
5. found
6. round

1. The hoop is round.
2. Mom needs some flour to make a cake.
3. He counted to fifty.

### Spelling List 25

1. bat
2. pet
3. self
4. out
5. our
6. round
7. mouth
8. **saw**
9. **put**
10. outside

Write an ‹ou› word and draw a picture in each house.

 **Action:** Pretend your finger is a needle and prick your thumb saying *ou, ou, ou.*

Spelling sheet 25

# Grammar 25 – Alphabetical order

*Prepare...*
*(Alphabet in four groups)*
*Write up examples*
*Dictionaries*
*Grammar sheet 25*

**Objective:** Develop the students' knowledge of the alphabet, and their ability to put words into alphabetical order.

**Introduction:** The students sit in a circle, and one student says the first letter of the alphabet. Go round the circle with each student saying the next letter. Then the students practice saying the alphabet in the four groups. They hold up one finger as they say the first group, pause, then hold up two fingers as they say the second, etc.

**Main point:** Write some words on the board. For simplicity, make sure each word begins with a different letter. With the students' help, put the words into alphabetical order. Then write a word on the board that the students will recognize even though it is deliberately mis-spelled, e.g. "momy." Ask if the word is spelled correctly. Tell the students that if they are not sure whether a spelling is correct, they can check it with a dictionary. Look up the word in the dictionary and read out the letters, asking the students to check the spelling on the board. Explain that if they do not know how a word is spelled, but can sound out the first few letters, then they will probably be able to find it in a dictionary.

**Grammar sheet 25:** The students put each group of words into alphabetical order. Then they write inside the outlined alphabet and look at the pictures at the bottom of the sheet. They try writing the word for each, and then check in a dictionary to see if they have spelled them correctly. Although the students may not know how to spell the word "television," they will probably be able to sound out the first few letters. If these words are not in the students' dictionaries then the pictures could be replaced, or the exercise could be treated as a whole-class activity, using one dictionary which does contain the words.

**Extension activity:** Draw pictures on the board. The students write words for the pictures and check their spellings in a dictionary.

**Finishing the lesson:** Go over the sheet with the students. Call out letters and see if the students can find the right section for them in the dictionary.

# Alphabetical Order

Put these words into alphabetical order.

1. car    truck    bus

_____    _____    _____

2. hamster    cat    rabbit

_____    _____    _____

3. lemon    apple    banana

_____    _____    _____

4. Sam    Mark    Rasheed    Greg

_____    _____    _____    _____

5. Emily    Lisa    Donna    Maria    Jennifer

_____    _____    _____    _____    _____

Look up the words for these nouns in your dictionary.
Copy the words out carefully.

_____            _____

A B C D E F G H I J K L M N O P Q R S T U V W X Y Z

Grammar sheet 25

# Spelling 26 – ‹ow›

**Review:** Review some basic sounds and the other spellings covered so far. Review tricky words "**any**," "**many**," "**more**," "**before**," "**other**," "**were**," "**because**," "**want**," "**saw**" and "**put**."

**Main point:** Remind the students that the main ways of writing the /ou/ sound are ‹ou› and ‹ow›. Review the ‹ow› spelling of the /ou/ sound. With the students, make a list of words which use it. Then ask them to make up sentences, using some of the words. The words could also be written onto a big owl shape.

**Spelling sheet 26:** The students write inside the outlined ow. Then in each owl they write an ‹ow› word and draw a picture for that word. Afterwards they color the sheet.

**Dictation:** Read the words and sentences for the students to write down. The Dictation Master on page 171 may be reproduced onto the back of the spelling sheets for the students to write on.

**Spelling list:** Read the spelling words with the students. In unison, call out the sounds in the regular words, and say the letter names for the tricky words "**could**" and "**should**." Both spellings can be learned with the mnemonic "**o u** lucky **d**uck." The longer word "flowerpot" is a compound word. It has three syllables and can be remembered as "flow," "er" and "pot," for spelling.

### Dictation

1. cow
2. now
3. clown
4. howl
5. crowd
6. powder

1. Come down here.
2. They went to town on the bus.
3. She had a quick shower.

### Spelling List 26

1. big
2. fox
3. mi**lk**
4. how
5. owl
6. brown
7. town
8. **could**
9. **should**
10. flowerpot

Use the words from our Spelling List to complete the sentences.

| | |
|---|---|
| once<br>upon<br>always<br>also<br>of<br>eight<br>love<br>cover<br>after<br>every<br>mother<br>father | 1. My _____ and _____ said I could have a pet.<br>2. _____ _____ a time, there was a mouse named Despereaux.<br>3. Please _____ your eyes so that I can get the surprise for you.<br>4. _____ morning I let the dogs outside. Of course I _____ let them in. _____ breakfast I let the horses out, too.<br>5. Do you _____ behave so nicely at school.<br>6. There are _____ baby ducks in the barn.<br>7. I know my parents _____ me.<br>8. How many _____ those cookies have you eaten. |

Use the words from our Spelling List to complete the sentences.

once
upon
always
also
of
eight
love
cover
after
every
mother
father

1. My _____ and _____ said I could have a pet.
2. _____ a time, there was a mouse named Despereaux.
3. Please _____ your eyes so that I can get the surprise for you.
4. _____ morning I let the dogs outside. Of course I _____ let them in. _____ breakfast I let the horses out, too.
5. Do you _____ behave so nicely at school.
6. There are _____ baby ducks in the barn.
7. I know my parents _____ me.
8. How many _____ those cookies have you eaten.

**Write an ‹ow› word and draw a picture in each owl.**

**Action:** Pretend your finger is a needle and prick your thumb saying *ou, ou, ou.*

# Grammar 26 – Verbs

**Objective:** Develop the students' understanding of verbs, and their ability to identify verbs in sentences.

**Introduction:** Review the parts of speech covered so far: proper and common nouns, pronouns, verbs and adjectives. Call out words for the students to do the appropriate actions. Remember that some words can function as both nouns and verbs, so the students can do both actions.

**Main point:** Review verbs. Look at the picture on Grammar sheet 26. Ask the students for examples of verbs. Remind them that if we can put the word "to" before a word, then it is probably a verb. Write some sentences on the board. Go through the sentences, finding the verbs with the students.

Examples:  The girls jump into the water.
           The dog chews his bone.

Underline the verbs in red.

**Grammar sheet 26:** The students look at the picture and write six verbs for the actions they can see. Then they read the sentences underneath and underline the verbs in red. Explain that there can be more than one verb in a sentence.

**Extension activity:** The students write some sentences about the picture and underline the verbs. The Writing Master on page 172 may be reproduced onto the back of the grammar sheets for the students to write on. The students could also look up their six verbs in the dictionary.

**Finishing the lesson:** Go over the sheet, with the students identifying the verbs.

# Verbs  Red

Write 6 verbs for actions you can see in the picture.

to _____   to _____

to _____   to _____

to _____   to _____

Underline the verbs in these sentences in red.
There can be more than one verb in a sentence.

1. Hannah smiled at her friend.

2. Carlos sails a boat.

3. Todd swims and dives in the sea.

4. The girls make a big sand castle and then play ball.

Grammar sheet 26

# Spelling 27 – ‹oi›

**Review:** Review some basic sounds and the other spellings covered so far. Review tricky words "**more**," "**before**," "**other**," "**were**," "**because**," "**want**," "**saw**," "**put**," "**could**" and "**should**."

**Main point:** Remind the students that the main ways of writing the /oi/ sound are ‹oi› and ‹oy›. Review the ‹oi› spelling of the /oi/ sound. With the students, make a list of words which use it. Then ask them to make up sentences, using some of the words. The words could also be written onto a big oil-can shape.

**Spelling sheet 27:** The students write inside the outlined oi. Then in each oil can they write an ‹oi› word, and draw a picture for that word. Afterwards they color the sheet.

**Dictation:** Read the words and sentences for the students to write down. The Dictation Master on page 171 may be reproduced onto the back of the spelling sheets for the students to write on.

**Spelling list:** Read the spelling words with the students. In unison, call out the sounds in the regular words, and say the letter names for the tricky words "**would**" and "**right**." "Would" can be learnt with the mnemonic "**o u** lucky **d**uck." "Right" is not really a tricky word, but the students need to remember that the /ie/ sound is made with the ‹igh› spelling. The longer word "boiling" has two syllables and can be remembered as "boil" and "ing" for spelling.

| Dictation | Spelling List 27 |
|---|---|
| 1. boil  4. joint | 1. bug |
| 2. join  5. foil | 2. had |
| 3. soil  6. spoil | 3. **film** |
|  | 4. oil |
|  | 5. coin |
| 1. It was a noisy car. | 6. noisy |
| 2. They are pointing at me. | 7. spoiled |
| 3. The snake was coiled. | 8. **would** |
|  | 9. **right** |
|  | 10. boiling |

Write an ‹oi› word and draw a picture in each oil can.

 **Action:** Cup hands around mouth and shout as if to another boat, *oi!, ship ahoy!*

Spelling sheet 27

# Grammar 27 – Adverbs

**Objective:** Develop the students' understanding of adverbs. Adverbs are words which describe verbs.

**Introduction:** Review verbs. Look at a picture showing lots of things happening. Ask the students for verbs for some of them. Make up some sentences using the verbs and write them on the board. Underline the verbs in red.

Examples:   They swim.
　　　　　　She sings.

**Main point:** Explain that just as adjectives describe nouns, there are also words which describe verbs. These words are called **adverbs**.

Action:　　　The action for an adverb is to bang one fist on top of the other.

Color:　　　 The color for adverbs is orange.

With the students, think of adverbs to describe the verbs in the sentences on the board, e.g. "They swim quickly," "She sings loudly." Underline the adverbs in orange.

**Grammar sheet 27:** The students read the adverbs at the top of the sheet and the unfinished sentences under the pictures. Then they decide which adverb could be used to complete each sentence. They can either copy the adverbs, or cut them out and stick them into the spaces provided.

**Extension activity:** Write some verbs on the board and ask the students to think of an adverb to describe each one.

Examples:　　speak　swim　sing　build　clean　paint　drive　play

**Finishing the lesson:** Go over the sheet with the students. Their answers are right as long as the adverbs chosen make sense in the sentences.

| slowly | loudly | hungrily |
|---|---|---|
| quickly | happily | secretly |

| slowly | loudly | hungrily |
|---|---|---|
| quickly | happily | secretly |

| slowly | loudly | hungrily |
|---|---|---|
| quickly | happily | secretly |

| slowly | loudly | hungrily |
|---|---|---|
| quickly | happily | secretly |

| slowly | loudly | hungrily |
|---|---|---|
| quickly | happily | secretly |

| slowly | loudly | hungrily |
|---|---|---|
| quickly | happily | secretly |

# Adverbs  🖉 Orange

Choose an adverb to go with each picture.

| secretly | happily | quickly |
|----------|---------|---------|
| hungrily | loudly  | slowly  |

Inky eats

Snake slithers

Bee buzzes

The ants whisper

Snail goes

The band played

**Action:** Bang one fist on top of the other.

**Color:** Orange

Grammar sheet 27

# Spelling 28 – ‹oy›

**Review:** Review some basic sounds and the other spellings covered so far. Review tricky words "**other**," "**were**," "**because**," "**want**," "**saw**," "**put**," "**could**," "**should**," "**would**" and "**right**."

**Main point:** Remind the students that the main ways of writing the /oi/ sound are ‹oi› and ‹oy›. Review the ‹**oy**› spelling of the /oi/ sound. Tell the students that the ‹oy› spelling is usually used at the end of words. The ‹y› takes the place of "shy ‹i›." The letter ‹i› does not like to be at the end of words. With the students, make a list of words which use ‹oy›. Then ask them to make up sentences, using some of the words. The words could also be written onto a big toy shape.

Examples:   boy      enjoy     annoy
            toy      destroy   royal
            joy      employ    loyal

**Spelling sheet 28:** The students write inside the outlined oy. Then in each toy they write an ‹oy› word and draw a picture for that word. Afterwards they color the sheet.

**Dictation:** Read the words and sentences for the students to write down. The Dictation Master on page 171 may be reproduced onto the back of the spelling sheets for the students to write on.

**Spelling list:** Read the spelling words with the students. In unison, call out the sounds in the regular words, and say the letter names for the tricky words "**two**" and "**four**." The longer word "destroy" has two syllables and can be remembered as "des" and "troy" for spelling.

## Dictation

1. boy
2. toy
3. joy
4. enjoy
5. royal
6. annoy

1. They enjoyed the trip.
2. The fly was annoying the boy.
3. Her toy car had a crash.

## Spelling List 28

1. jet
2. dig
3. he**lp**
4. boy
5. toy
6. enjoy
7. annoy
8. **two**
9. **four**
10. destroy

**Write an ‹oy› word and draw a picture in each toy.**

 **Action:** Cup hands around mouth and shout as if to another boat, *oi!, ship ahoy!*

# Grammar 28 – Adverbs

**Objective:** Develop the students' understanding of adverbs.

**Introduction:** Review verbs. Talk about Inky, Snake and Bee (or some of the students). With the students, decide where they might go for an outing, e.g. to the park or to the beach. Think of things they might do, e.g. climb up the slide or build a sand castle. Make a list of these activities on the board.

**Main point:** Review adverbs. With the students, think of some adverbs to describe the verbs listed on the board.

**Grammar sheet 28:** The students read the adverbs at the top of the sheet, and the story in the beehive. Then they decide which adverb could be used to fill each gap.

**Extension activity:** The students write, or draw a picture, about what they think Inky, Snake and Bee might do on their day out. The Writing Master on page 172 may be reproduced onto the back of the grammar sheets for the students to write on.

**Finishing the lesson:** Go over the sheet with the students. Their answers are right as long as the adverbs chosen make sense in the sentences. Ask the students where they think Inky, Snake and Bee went.

# Adverbs

Read these adverbs, then read the story in the beehive.
Write an adverb in each space.

| loudly | soon | suddenly |
|--------|------|----------|
| quickly | happily | slowly |

### Bee's Busy Day

Bee woke up _____, and crawled _____ down the hive to have breakfast. She buzzed _____ as she flew to the farm. She _____ collected as much pollen as she could, and flew _____ back to the hive. She smiled _____ to herself. Bee and her friends, Inky and Snake, had planned a day out.

# Spelling 29 – ‹ar›

Prepare...
Flash cards:
• basic sounds
• new spellings
• tricky words
Spelling sheet 29
Spelling list 29
Star shape

**Review:** Review some basic sounds and the other spellings covered so far. Review tricky words "**because**," "**want**," "**saw**," "**put**," "**could**," "**should**," "**would**," "**right**," "**two**" and "**four**."

**Main point:** The ‹ar› spelling can be pronounced in two different ways, either as /ah/, or with an audible /r/ at the end. In regions where the ‹r› is not sounded, remind the students that the main ways of writing the /ar/ sound are ‹ar›, ‹al›, ‹au› and ‹aw›. In regions where the /r/ is clearly pronounced, it is important that the students also learn the /ah/ sound, as made by ‹al›, ‹au› and ‹aw›.

Review the ‹ar› spelling of the /ar/ sound. With the students, make a list of words which use it. Then ask them to make up sentences, using some of the words. The words could also be written onto a big star shape.

**Spelling sheet 6:** The students write inside the outlined ar. Then in each star they write an ‹ar› word and draw a picture for that word. Afterwards they color the sheet.

**Dictation:** Read the words and sentences for the students to write down. Tell the students that the /k/ sound at the end of "park" and "shark" is a "kicking ‹k›." Later they will learn rules to help them choose between ‹c›, ‹k› and ‹ck›. The Dictation Master on page 171 may be reproduced onto the back of the spelling sheets for the students to write on.

**Spelling list:** Read the spelling words with the students. In unison, call out the sounds in the regular words, and say the letter names for the tricky words "**goes**" and "**does**." Point out to the students that "are" is only tricky because they must remember to put the ‹e› on the end. The longer word "barnyard" is a compound word. It has two syllables and can be remembered as "barn" and "yard" for spelling.

## Dictation

1. car
2. jar
3. part
4. start
5. shark
6. march

1. She drives a red car.
2. I ran all the way to the park.
3. Sharks have very sharp teeth.

## Spelling List 29

1. got
2. bun
3. belt
4. arm
5. hard
6. scarf
7. cart
8. **goes**
9. **does**
10. barnyard

Write an ‹**ar**› word and draw a picture in each star.

 **Action:** Open mouth wide and say *ah*, as if at the doctor.

 **Alternative action:** Flap hands as if a seal, and say *ar, ar, ar.*

Spelling sheet 29

# Grammar 29 – ‹es› Plurals

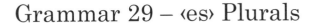

**Prepare...**
(Jolly Grammar Big Book 1)
Write up examples
Grammar sheet 29
(Scissors)
(Stapler)

**Objective:** Develop the students' understanding of singular and plural, and their knowledge that, if a word ends in ‹sh›, ‹ch›, ‹s› or ‹x›, the plural is made by adding ‹es›.

**Introduction:** Review singular and plural. Write some sentences on the board.

Examples:  The dog barked loudly.
           The cat walked slowly.

With the students, identify the parts of speech and underline them in the appropriate colors. Then ask the students to make the nouns plural.

**Main point:** Tell the students that if a word ends in ‹sh›, ‹ch›, ‹s› or ‹x›, then the plural is made by adding **‹es›**.

| Examples: | wish | church | dress | box |
|---|---|---|---|---|
| | dish | bunch | kiss | fox |
| | crash | catch | cross | six |
| | brush | ditch | class | fix |

**Grammar sheet 29:** The students write inside the outlined letters in the left-hand boxes. Then they choose a noun for each spelling and write it in the central box. They write the plural of the noun in the right-hand box and draw a picture for each word. Remind the students that the picture for each plural must show more than one item. They can cut their sheets as indicated and put the four sections in a pile. Each pile can be stapled on the dotted line on the left-hand side, to make a little book with the ‹sh› on top. Fold the four pages as indicated, so they can be unfolded to reveal "brush" and "brushes," etc.

**Extension activity:** Write some sentences on the board which use nouns in the singular. Ask the students to write the sentences in the plural. Either use only ‹es› plurals, or mix them up with regular ‹s› plurals. Alternatively the students could think of as many words as they can that end with ‹sh›, ‹ch›, ‹s› or ‹x›.

**Finishing the lesson:** Call out some nouns, some of which need ‹es› and some of which need ‹s› to make the plural. The students listen carefully to each word and say which letter(s) should be added.

‹es› plurals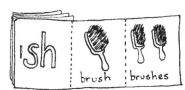

| sh | brush | brushes |
| ch | | |
| s | | |
| x | | |

Grammar sheet 29

# Spelling 30 – ‹al›

**Review:** Review some basic sounds and the other spellings covered so far. Review tricky words "**saw**," "**put**," "**could**," "**should**," "**would**," "**right**," "**two**," "**four**," "**goes**" and "**does**."

**Main point:** The ‹ar› spelling can be pronounced in two different ways, either as /ah/, or with an audible /r/ at the end. In regions where the ‹r› is not sounded, remind the students that the main ways of writing the /ar/ sound are ‹ar›, ‹al›, ‹au› and ‹aw›. In regions where the /r/ is clearly pronounced, it is important that the students also learn the /ah/ sound, as made by ‹al›, ‹au› and ‹aw›.

Review the ‹al› spelling of the /ar/ sound. With the students, make a list of words which use it. Then ask them to make up sentences, using some of the words. The words could also be written onto a talk-bubble shape.

**Spelling sheet 30:** The students write inside the outlined al. Then in each talk bubble they write an ‹al› word and draw a picture for that word. Afterwards they color the sheet.

**Dictation:** Read the words and sentences for the students to write down. The Dictation Master on page 171 may be reproduced onto the back of the spelling sheets for the students to write on.

**Spelling list:** Read the spelling words with the students. In unison, call out the sounds in the regular words, and say the letter names for the tricky words "**made**" and "**their**." "Made" is not really a tricky word, but the students need to remember that the /ai/ sound is made with the ‹a_e› spelling. For "their," tell the students that this spelling is used for belonging, e.g. "their clothes," "their toys." The longer word "beanstalk" is a compound word. It has two syllables and can be remembered as "bean" and "stalk" for spelling.

## Dictation

1. also
2. talk
3. always
4. falling
5. ball
6. wall

1. They took a short walk.
2. She always hit the ball.
3. All the stalks grew tall.

## Spelling List 30

1. bad
2. vet
3. **fact**
4. all
5. talk
6. walk
7. small
8. **made**
9. **their**
10. beanstalk

Write an ‹al› word and draw a picture in each talk bubble.

**Action:** Open mouth wide and say *ah*, as if at the doctor.

Spelling sheet 30

# Grammar 30 – Antonyms

**Objective:** Develop the students' understanding of antonyms, which is another word for opposites.

**Introduction:** Give a few examples of antonyms, or opposites, e.g. "big/small," "dark/light," "up/down." Call out some words and ask for their antonyms. Then see if the students can suggest any antonym pairs themselves.

**Main point:** Write some sentences on the board and read them with the students.

Example: A tall man drove backwards out of his garage and onto a rough road. At the corner he turned right. It was a dark, wet night. He made a quick turn at a small bend in the road and hit a low wall. The car went over the wall and stopped.

With the students, identify those words which have antonyms. Try putting the antonyms into the sentences and see if the story still makes sense.

**Grammar sheet 30:** The students read each word, and write its antonym on the line in the opposite half of the box. They draw a picture for each antonym.

**Extension activity:** Write some jumbled antonyms on the board, for the students to identify the pairs, and write them down. Alternatively the antonyms could be written on cards for the students to sort into pairs.

Examples:
| | | |
|---|---|---|
| backwards/forwards | right/wrong | good/bad |
| rough/smooth | sharp/blunt | fat/thin |
| near/far | easy/hard | wet/dry |
| slow/quick | right/left | high/low |
| dark/light | over/under | small/large |
| long/short | liquid/solid | little/big |

**Finishing the lesson:** Call out some phrases or sentences which use words with antonyms. Ask the students to identify those words and to replace them with their antonyms, e.g. "a big dog"/"a small dog"; "He walked slowly."/"He walked quickly."; "an easy sum"/"a hard sum."

# Opposites       Antonyms

Write each opposite and draw a picture.

white

day

hot

quiet

up

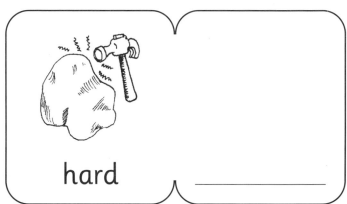
hard

asleep

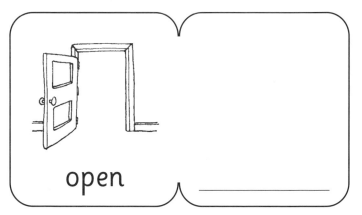
open

Grammar sheet 30

# Spelling 31 – ‹nk›

**Review:** Review some basic sounds and the other spellings covered so far. Review tricky words "**could**," "**should**," "**would**," "**right**," "**two**," "**four**," "**goes**," "**does**," "**made**" and "**their**."

**Main point:** Introduce the ‹nk› spelling of the combined sounds /ng/ and /k/. When together, these sounds are nearly always written as ‹nk›, so this is an important spelling pattern to learn. With the students, make a list of words which use ‹nk›. Then ask them to make up sentences, using some of the words. The words could also be written onto a big drink shape.

**Spelling sheet 31:** The students write inside the outlined nk. Then in each drink they write an ‹nk› word, and draw a picture for that word. Afterwards they color the sheet.

**Dictation:** Read the words and sentences for the students to write down. The Dictation Master on page 171 may be reproduced onto the back of the spelling sheets for the students to write on.

**Spelling list:** Read the spelling words with the students. In unison, call out the sounds in the regular words, and say the letter names for the tricky words "**once**" and "**upon**." The longer word "thinking" has two syllables and can be remembered as "think" and "ing" for spelling.

### Dictation

1. ink
2. rink
3. blink
4. trunk
5. drank
6. shrink

1. The pink pig blinked.
2. What would you like to drink?
3. I sleep in the top bunk.

### Spelling List 31

1. fin
2. sob
3. left
4. sink
5. pink
6. drink
7. thank
8. **once**
9. **upon**
10. thinking

Write an ‹**nk**› word and draw a picture in each drink.

Spelling sheet 31

# Grammar 31 – Alphabetical order

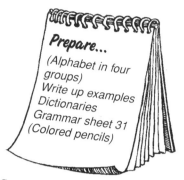

**Objective:** Develop the students' knowledge of the alphabet, and their ability to use word books and dictionaries.

**Introduction:** The students sit in a circle and say the letters of the alphabet in turn. Then they practice saying the alphabet in the four groups. They hold up one finger as they say the first group, pause, then hold up two fingers as they say the second, etc. Call out letters. Ask the students which group each letter belongs to, e.g. "s" is in group 3. Knowing where a letter falls in the alphabet will help the students work out where to look for it in the dictionary. Call out a letter and ask the students to say which letter comes before it and which after it. Repeat with other letters.

**Main point:** Tell the students that they can use a dictionary to help them if they are not sure how a word is spelled. Explain that they will need to sound out the first few letters of the word, find the appropriate section of the dictionary, and then look for the word. If they have already written a word but decide that it looks wrong, they can check the spelling by looking up the word in the dictionary.

Write a few words on the board, mis-spelling some of them. (Make sure all the words are included in the dictionaries used.)

Examples:    leter    animal    coocky

Ask the students whether they think the words are spelled correctly. Then look the words up in a dictionary and correct them with the students.

**Grammar sheet 31:** There are two spellings underneath each picture. The students read them, then look up the word in the dictionary, and tick the correct spelling. The three words in the middle have been mis-spelled. The students look up these words and correct the spellings. They can use colored pencils to make their corrections clear. Then the students look up the last two words on the sheet, and copy out the meanings given in their dictionaries. Make sure all the words are included in the dictionaries used. If a word is not included, replace it with one that is.

**Extension activity:** Write some more words on the board and ask the students to find out what they mean. The words could be related to a topic the students are studying.

**Finishing the lesson:** Go over the sheet with the students, checking the spellings and meanings of the words.

# Using a Dictionary

You can use a dictionary to check how to spell words.
Look up each word in your dictionary to choose the right spelling.

toofbrush
toothbrush

rabbit
rabit

starr
star

octopus
octapus

flouer
flower

buterfie
butterfly

These words are spelled wrongly. Look them up and copy them correctly.

**boock**  **carpit**  **triangel**

_____   _____   _____

You can also use a dictionary to find the meaning of a word.
Look up these words and write down what they mean.

**atlas** _____

_____

**yacht** _____

_____

Grammar sheet 31

# Spelling 32 – ‹er›

**Review:** Review some basic sounds and the other spellings covered so far. Review tricky words "**would**," "**right**," "**two**," "**four**," "**goes**," "**does**," "**made**," "**their**," "**once**" and "**upon**."

**Main point:** Remind the students that the main ways of writing the /er/ sound are ‹er›, ‹ir› and ‹ur›. Review the ‹er› spelling of the /er/ sound. The ‹er› spelling often comes at the end of words, where it makes a slightly shorter sound. With the students, make a list of words which use it. Then ask them to make up sentences, using some of the words. The words could also be written onto a big gingerbread shape.

**Spelling sheet 32:** The students write inside the outlined er. Then in each gingerbread person they write an ‹er› word, and draw a picture for that word. Afterwards they color the sheet.

**Dictation:** Read the words and sentences for the students to write down. The Dictation Master on page 171 may be reproduced onto the back of the spelling sheets for the students to write on.

**Spelling list:** Read the spelling words with the students. In unison, call out the sounds in the regular words, and say the letter names for the tricky words "**always**" and "**also**." It may help to tell the students that when "all" is part of a compound word, it loses the second ‹l›. The longer word "woodpecker" is also a compound word. It has three syllables and can be remembered as "wood," "peck" and "er," for spelling.

### Dictation

1. fern
2. term
3. perch
4. never
5. winter
6. silver

1. He was very stern.
2. Her ring is made of silver.
3. There are fish in the river.

### Spelling List 32

1. mud
2. jam
3. s**en**t
4. herd
5. summer
6. river
7. number
8. **always**
9. **also**
10. woodpecker

Write an ‹er› word and draw a picture in each gingerbread person.

**Action:** Roll hands over each other like a mixer and say *ererer*.

Spelling sheet 32

# Grammar 32 – Speech Marks

**Objective:** Develop the students' understanding of speech marks.

**Introduction:** Find a comic or book which uses speech bubbles. Ask the students what the speech bubbles are for. Read some of the speech in the bubbles. Draw a speech bubble on the board. Draw an animal or write its name. Ask the students what noise the animal makes. Write this in the speech bubble. Ask the students to think of some more animals and the sounds they make. Write some of these sounds in the speech bubble on the board.

**Main Point:** Now show the students a page of a book which has speech marks. Point out the speech marks and see if the students can say why they are there. Point out that the first word after the speech marks usually has a capital letter. Explain that the speech marks are used before and after anything that is actually spoken. The words that come out of our mouths are called "speech" and it is only these words that go between the speech marks. It may help the students write the speech marks correctly, if they think of them as a "66" before the speech and a "99" after it. Read aloud from the book, with the students looking out for speech marks and reading the spoken words themselves.

**Grammar sheet 32:** The students write in the outlined speech marks. Then they think what noise each animal makes, e.g. "Hiss" for the snake. They write the noise, first in the speech bubble and then in the box underneath. Remind them to start each one with a capital letter. In the first two examples, the speech marks are provided in outline. In the others, the students should write the speech marks themselves, in the circles provided.

**Extension activity:** Write some sentences on the board. The students copy the sentences and put in the speech marks.

Examples:   Bow wow said the dog.
My cat is called Tolly said Dan.
The girl said I like going to the beach.

**Finishing the lesson:** Go over the sheet, with the students suggesting the sounds the animals might make. If there are sentences on the board, go over them, with the students adding the speech marks.

# "Speech Marks"

said the snake.

said the cow.

said the bird.

said the bee.

said the duck.

said the donkey.

Grammar sheet 32

# Spelling 33 – ‹ir›

**Review:** Review some basic sounds and the other spellings covered so far. Review tricky words "**two**," "**four**," "**goes**," "**does**," "**made**," "**their**," "**once**," "**upon**," "**always**" and "**also**."

**Main point:** Remind the students that the main ways of writing the /er/ sound are ‹er›, ‹ir› and ‹ur›. Review the ‹ir› spelling of the /er/ sound. With the students, make a list of words which use it. Then ask them to make up sentences, using some of the words. The words could also be written onto a big bird shape. Tell the students that an /er/ sound in a number word will probably be spelt ‹ir›, e.g. "first," "third," "thirteen" and "thirty."

**Spelling sheet 33:** The students write inside the outlined ir. Then in each bird they write an ‹ir› word, and draw a picture for that word. Afterwards they color the sheet.

**Dictation:** Read the words and sentences for the students to write down. The Dictation Master on page 171 may be reproduced onto the back of the spelling sheets for the students to write on.

**Spelling list:** Read the spelling words with the students. In unison, call out the sounds in the regular words, and say the letter names for the tricky words "**of**" and "**eight**." Remind the students to write "of" with an ‹f›, although it has a /v/ sound at the end. The longer word "birthday" is a compound word. It has two syllables and can be remembered as "birth" and "day" for spelling.

## Dictation

1. dirt
2. stir
3. sir
4. third
5. thirty
6. bird

1. The girl was thirsty.
2. When is your birthday?
3. I have a green skirt and a red shirt.

## Spelling List 33

1. yet
2. hid
3. ke**pt**
4. skirt
5. girl
6. shirt
7. first
8. **of**
9. **eight**
10. birthday

**Write an ‹ir› word and draw a picture in each bird.**

 **Action:** Roll hands over each other like a mixer and say *erererer*.

Spelling sheet 33

# Grammar 33 – Word Web

**Objective:** Encourage the students to think about the words they choose in their writing.

**Introduction:** Explain that some words can have the same or similar meanings as each other, e.g. "bad," "horrible," "terrible" and "awful." Ask the students if they can think of any other words which mean "bad." Then ask if they can think of similar meanings for other words.

Examples:   happy   sad   hot   dirty   small   big   hurry

The students could also be shown a thesaurus. Explain that it is a special book which tells us about words with similar meanings.

**Main Point:** Tell the students that they can make their writing more interesting by thinking carefully about the words they use, and by avoiding using the same word over and over again. One word which is often overused is "said." Write a sentence on the board, reminding the students about speech marks.

Example:   "Where are you going?" said Jim.

Encourage the students to think of the different ways Jim might say this, and the different words they could use.

Examples:
| asked | replied | called | shouted | cried |
| whispered | roared | murmured | explained | yelled |
| screamed | answered | muttered | wondered | hissed |

**Grammar sheet 33:** The students write a word that could be used instead of "said," in each section of the word web. They could look in books to find more examples.

**Extension activity:** Let the students look at, and read, some thesauruses.

**Finishing the lesson:** See how many different words the students have thought of, or found. Make a class collection on a big "word web."

# Word Web

How many words can you think of that you could use instead of "said"? Write the words in the spaces of the word web.

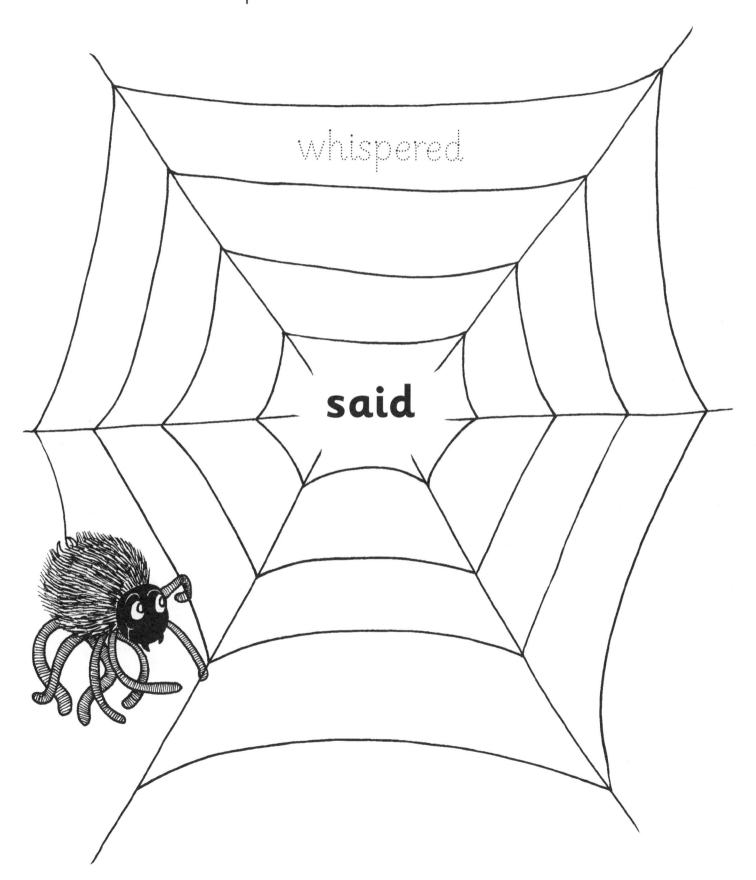

Grammar sheet 33

# Spelling 34 – ‹ur›

**Prepare...**
Flash cards:
• basic sounds
• new spellings
• tricky words
Spelling sheet 34
Spelling list 34
Turkey shape

**Review:** Review some basic sounds and the other spellings covered so far. Review tricky words "**goes**," "**does**," "**made**," "**their**," "**once**," "**upon**," "**always**," "**also**," "**of**" and "**eight**."

**Main point:** Remind the students that the main ways of writing the /er/ sound are ‹er›, ‹ir› and ‹ur›. Review the ‹ur› spelling of the /er/ sound. With the students, make a list of words which use it. Then ask them to make up sentences, using some of the words. The words could also be written onto a big turkey shape. Tell the students that two days of the week take the ‹ur› spelling: "Saturday" and "Thursday."

**Spelling sheet 34:** The students write inside the outlined ur. Then in each turkey they write a ‹ur› word, and draw a picture for that word. Afterwards they color the sheet.

**Dictation:** Read the words and sentences for the students to write down. The Dictation Master on page 171 may be reproduced onto the back of the spelling sheets for the students to write on.

**Spelling list:** Read the spelling words with the students. In unison, call out the sounds in the regular words, and say the letter names for the tricky words "**love**" and "**cover**." The longer word "hamburger" is a compound word. It has three syllables and can be remembered as "ham," "bur" and "ger," for spelling. Point out that the /er/ sound in the middle of the word is spelt ‹ur›, but the /er/ sound at the end is spelt ‹er›.

## Dictation

1. fur
2. burn
3. hurt
4. burst
5. curly
6. turning

1. The nurse visited on Thursday.
2. We always have burnt toast.
3. It is your turn next.

## Spelling List 34

1. not
2. sum
3. ne**x**t
4. turn
5. nurse
6. turkey
7. purple
8. **love**
9. **cover**
10. hamburger

Write a ‹ur› word and draw a picture in each turkey.

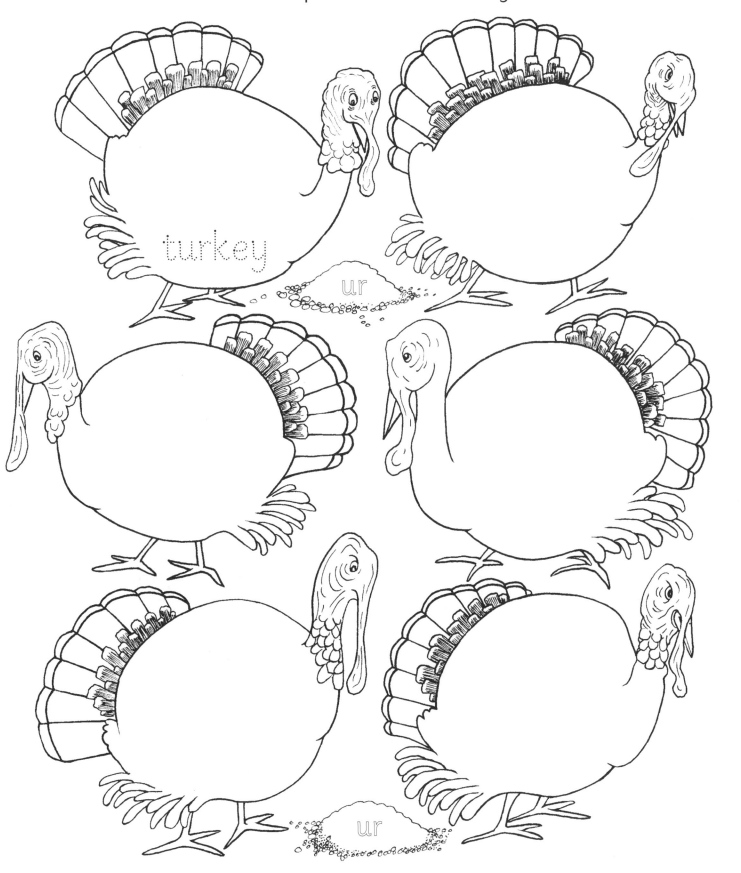

 **Action:** Roll hands over each other like a mixer and say *ererer*.

Spelling sheet 34

# Grammar 34 – Questions

**Objective:** Develop the students' understanding of questions, and of when to use question marks.

**Introduction:** Sit the students in a circle. Have the months of the year written out, for the students to see. Read them with the students. Go round the circle, with each student in turn saying the next month. Then go round the circle, asking each student "When is your birthday?"

**Main Point:** Write the question "When is your birthday?" on the board. Ask the students if they know what the mark at the end of the sentence is. Explain that it is a question mark and that it tells us that the sentence is a question. Demonstrate how to write a question mark. Write the ‹wh› question words on the board: "what," "why," "when," "where," "who" and "which." Read the words with the students. Usually when we ask a question, we expect an answer, as questions can be used to get information. The students learned when each others' birthdays were by asking the question "When is your birthday?" Ask them to imagine meeting someone for the first time. What other questions could they ask, to find out more about that person?

**Grammar sheet 34:** With the students, go through the sheet, reading the question words. The students write inside the outlined question words and the ?, using colored pencils if they prefer. Remind them to start the question marks at the top. Next they answer the three questions about themselves. Then they think of some questions they could ask someone they had just met for the first time, to find out more about that person.

**Extension activity:** The students think of as many questions as they can. Then they could take turns asking questions with a partner.

**Finishing the lesson:** Go round the class, asking the students for their questions.

# Questions

## Question words

what  why  when
where  who  which

Go over the question marks, using different colors.

? ? ? ? ? ? ? ? ? ?

Answer these questions.

1. What is your name?  _____  _____

2. Where do you live?  _____

3. When is your birthday?  _____

? ? ? ? ? ? ? ? ? ?

If you met someone for the first time, what other questions could you ask?

_____

_____

_____

_____

Grammar sheet 34

# Spelling 35 – ‹au›

**Review:** Review some basic sounds and the other spellings covered so far. Review tricky words "**made**," "**their**," "**once**," "**upon**," "**always**," "**also**," "**of**," "**eight**," "**love**" and "**cover**."

**Main point:** The ‹ar› spelling can be pronounced in two different ways, either as /ah/, or with an audible /r/ at the end. In regions where the ‹r› is not sounded, remind the students that the main ways of writing the /ar/ sound are ‹ar›, ‹al›, ‹au› and ‹aw›. In regions where the /r/ is clearly pronounced, it is important that the students also learn the /ah/ sound, as made by ‹al›, ‹au› and ‹aw›.

Review the ‹au› spelling of the /ar/ sound. With the students, make a list of words which use it. Then ask them to make up sentences, using some of the words. The words could also be written onto a big astronaut shape.

Examples:   haul      haunt       fault      pause
            laundry   astronaut   Autumn     August

**Spelling sheet 35:** The students write inside the outlined au. Then in each astronaut they write an ‹au› word, and draw a picture for that word. Afterwards they color the sheet.

**Dictation:** Read the words and sentences for the students to write down. The Dictation Master on page 171 may be reproduced onto the back of the spelling sheets for the students to write on.

**Spelling list:** Read the spelling words with the students. In unison, call out the sounds in the regular words, and say the letter names for the tricky words "**after**" and "**every**." The longer word "astronaut" has three syllables and can be remembered as "as," "tron" and "aut," for spelling.

| Dictation | Spelling List 35 |
|---|---|
| 1. haul   4. August | 1. map |
| 2. fault  5. launch | 2. fix |
| 3. haunt  6. vault | 3. ju**mp** |
|  | 4. fault |
|  | 5. autumn |
| 1. They always go there in August. | 6. haunt |
| 2. It was her fault. | 7. August |
| 3. Once I saw an astronaut. | 8. **after** |
|  | 9. **every** |
|  | 10. astronaut |

Write an ‹au› word and draw a picture in each astronaut.

  **Action:** Open mouth wide and say *ah*, as if at the doctor.

# Grammar 35 – Questions

**Objective:** Develop the students' understanding and use of questions.

**Introduction:** Ask the students some questions, e.g. "What is your favorite color?" "Where did you go on holiday?" "Who is your best friend?" "When is your birthday?" "Which drink do you like better – orange or grape?" Review the ‹wh› question words, and write them on the board: "what," "why," "when," "where," "who" and "which."

Write questions on the board, with the question words missing.

Examples:　　　_____ do you live?　　　　(Missing word: "where")
　　　　　　　_____ does your party start?　(Missing word: "when")
　　　　　　　_____ likes chocolate?　　　　(Missing word: "who")

Ask which question word would fit in each sentence. With the students, try inserting each of the question words in turn, to find one that makes sense.

**Main Point:** Show the students pictures of animals. Ask one student to choose an animal, but not to say which it is. The others ask questions to find out which animal it is. Remind the students that questions are usually asked to get information. The students will need to think carefully about which questions to ask, to find out as much as possible about the animal. They must not guess which it is, until five questions have been asked. This is a simplified version of the game "20 questions," and the rules can be adapted to suit the class. It can be played in spare moments, and can become more like "20 questions" as the students improve at asking questions.

**Grammar sheet 35:** Read through the sheet with the students. They choose a ‹wh› question word that makes sense to complete each of the questions. Then they read the questions and answers underneath, to work out which animal has been chosen.

**Extension activity:** The students play the animal game in pairs.

**Finishing the lesson:** Go over the sheet with the students.

# Questions

You ask questions to find things out.

what   why   when   where   who   which

Choose a question word to fit the sentences.

1. _____ won the quiz?

2. _____ time is it?

3. _____ book do you like best?

4. _____ are you going on holiday?

5. _____ did you do that?

6. _____ can we play basketball?

Read the questions and answers. See if you can guess which animal this is.

1. Do you have fur?                Yes
2. How many legs do you have?      Four
3. What do you eat?                Carrots and grass
4. Do you have long ears?          Yes

Which animal is it? _____

Find a partner and play the game yourself.

Grammar sheet 35

# Spelling 36 – ‹aw›

**Review:** Review some basic sounds and the other spellings. Review tricky words "**once**," "**upon**," "**always**," "**also**," "**of**," "**eight**," "**love**," "**cover**," "**after**" and "**every**."

**Main point:** The ‹ar› spelling can be pronounced in two different ways, either as /ah/, or with an audible /r/ at the end. In regions where the ‹r› is not sounded, remind the students that the main ways of writing the /ar/ sound are ‹ar›, ‹al›, ‹au› and ‹aw›. In regions where the /r/ is clearly pronounced, it is important that the students also learn the /ah/ sound, as made by ‹al›, ‹au› and ‹aw›.

Review the ‹**aw**› spelling of the /ar/ sound. With the students, make a list of words which use it. Then ask them to make up sentences, using some of the words. The words could also be written onto a big saw shape.

Examples:
| | | | | |
|---|---|---|---|---|
| saw | law | paw | jaw | raw |
| claw | flaw | straw | draw | hawk |
| dawn | prawn | yawn | crawl | awful |

**Spelling sheet 36:** The students write inside the outlined aw. Then in each saw they write an ‹aw› word and draw a picture for that word. Afterwards they color the sheet.

**Dictation:** Read the words and sentences for the students to write down. The Dictation Master on page 171 may be reproduced onto the back of the spelling sheets for the students to write on.

**Spelling list:** Read the spelling words with the students. In unison, call out the sounds in the regular words, and say the letter names for the tricky words "**mother**" and "**father**." The longer word "strawberry" is a compound word. It has three syllables and can be remembered as "straw," "ber" and "ry," for spelling.

### Dictation

1. raw
2. claw
3. thaw
4. yawn
5. shawl
6. straw

1. I have drawn a picture.
2. The cows lay down on some straw.
3. Would you like some prawns?

### Spelling List 36

1. zip
2. men
3. po**nd**
4. saw
5. claw
6. dawn
7. prawn
8. **mother**
9. **father**
10. strawberry

**Write an ‹aw› word and draw a picture in each saw.**

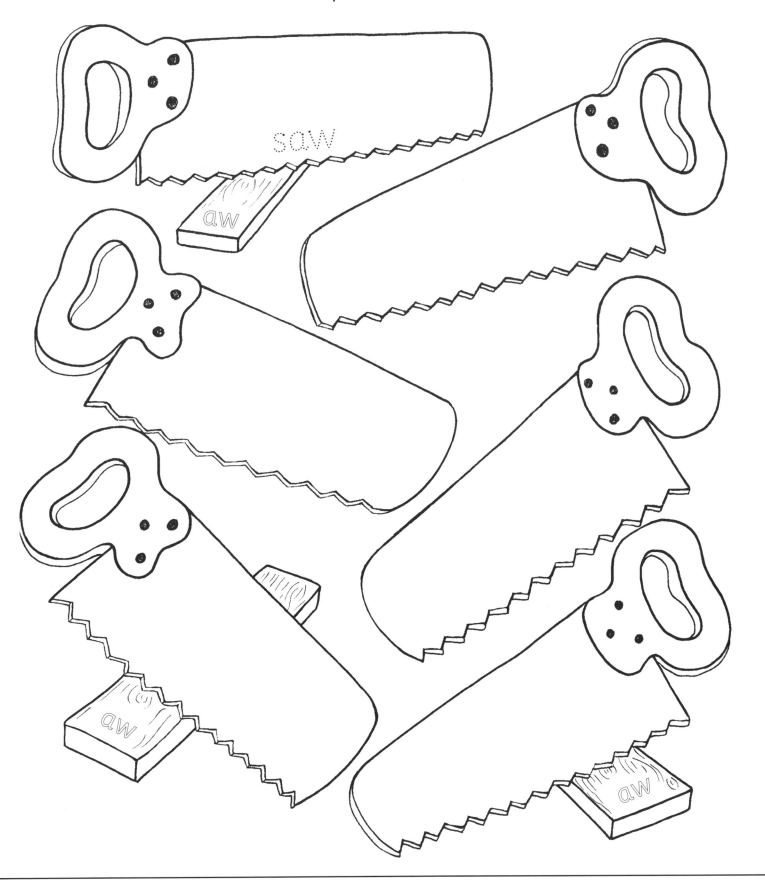

 **Action:** Open mouth wide and say *ah*, as if at the doctor.

# Grammar 36 – Review

**Objective:** Review the parts of speech learned so far.

**Introduction:** Review proper nouns, common nouns and pronouns. Review adjectives. Call out some nouns and ask the students to think of adjectives to describe them. Review verbs. Conjugate a verb. Call out some verbs and ask the students to think of adverbs to describe them.

**Main Point:** This is a review session, allowing the students to apply some of what they have learned, to a piece of writing. Choose a page from a big book and read it, with the students identifying the parts of speech they have learned. A large sheet of acetate could be placed over the page, and used to underline the words in the appropriate colors.

**Grammar sheet 36:** With the students, read the story on the sheet. (This same sheet can be shown in large format from the *Jolly Grammar Big Book 1.*) First the students write inside the word, nouns, in black, and underline all the nouns they can find. Then they repeat for the verbs, underlining in red. It does not matter if the students do not find all the nouns and verbs, as long as they see some of them and show that they are beginning to understand how words work in sentences.

**Extension activity:** The students repeat the exercise, looking for the pronouns, adjectives and adverbs.

**Finishing the lesson:** Go over the sheet with the students. (See answers below.)
Key: Noun$^N$  Verb$^V$  Pronoun$^P$  Adjective$^{Adj}$  Adverb$^{Adv}$

"Inky$^N$ works$^V$ hard$^{Adv}$ in the garden$^N$. She$^P$ digs$^V$ the brown$^{Adj}$ earth$^N$. The birds$^N$ watch$^V$ her interestedly$^{Adv}$. They$^P$ wait$^V$ impatiently$^{Adv}$ for the worms$^N$.

In the Spring$^N$ she$^P$ plants$^V$ the seeds$^N$ in the ground$^N$. She$^P$ grows$^V$ orange$^{Adj}$ carrots$^N$, crispy$^{Adj}$ lettuces$^N$ and tall$^{Adj}$, green$^{Adj}$ beans$^N$. In Summer$^N$, she$^P$ carefully$^{Adv}$ harvests$^V$ the delicious$^{Adj}$ vegetables$^N$ and eats$^V$ them.

She$^P$ also grows$^V$ tall$^{Adj}$, yellow$^{Adj}$ sunflowers$^N$. She$^P$ likes$^V$ the beautiful$^{Adj}$ sunflowers$^N$. The birds$^N$ also$^{Adv}$ like$^V$ the sunflowers$^N$. They$^P$ hungrily$^{Adv}$ eat$^V$ the striped$^{Adj}$ black$^{Adj}$ and white$^{Adj}$ seeds$^N$."

Nouns — Black    Verbs — Red

Underline the nouns in black and the verbs in red.

Inky works hard in the garden. She digs the brown earth. The birds watch her interestedly. They wait impatiently for the worms.

In the Spring she plants the seeds in the ground. She grows orange carrots, crispy lettuces and tall, green beans. In Summer, she carefully harvests the delicious vegetables and eats them.

She also grows tall, yellow sunflowers. She likes the beautiful sunflowers. The birds also like the sunflowers. They hungrily eat the striped black and white seeds.

Pronouns — Pink    Adjectives — Blue    Adverbs — Orange

Now see if you can underline the pronouns in pink, the adjectives in blue, and the adverbs in orange.

*Reproducible Section 2*

# Master Sheets

Dictation Master (page 171)

This master may be reproduced onto the back of the Spelling Sheets. It provides lines for the students to write the dictation words and sentences.

Writing Master (page 172)

This master may be reproduced on to the back of the Grammar Sheets, when required. It provides extra lines which the students may need for their writing.

Parts of Speech Master (page 173)

This master may be reproduced and enlarged to make a poster for display in the classroom. The names of the parts of speech are provided in outline, to be filled in with the appropriate colors.

Name: _____

# Dictation

1. _____    2. _____

3. _____    4. _____

5. _____    6. _____

# Sentences

1. _____

   _____

2. _____

   _____

3. _____

   _____

Name: _____

# Parts of Speech

## Nouns — Black

## Pronouns — Pink

## Verbs — Red

## Adjectives — Blue

## Adverbs — Orange

# Reproducible Section 3

# *Flash Card Sheets*

There are two sets of sheets which may be reproduced, cut up, and pasted onto card to make flash cards.

Digraphs and Alternative Vowel Spellings (pages 175-80)

At this stage the students should already know the sounds made by the single alphabet letters. They will, however, take longer to master the digraphs (two letters which make a single sound), and will need to learn the alternative ways of spelling vowel sounds. Go through the flash cards as often as possible.

Consonant Blends (pages 181-85)

It is difficult for students to hear the individual sounds in consonant blends (clusters of two or more consonants). It is useful for them to know these blends well.

Students read unfamiliar words with greater ease once they can blend consonants together fluently, instead of sounding out each one on its own, e.g. "**fl**-a-p," not "f-l-a-p." Hold up each flash card for the students to say the blend.

For writing, students need to be aware of the individual sounds in a blend. They often write a word like "flap" as "fap," because they do not hear the second sound in the blend. This problem can be overcome with regular practice. Call out blends, for the students to say the individual sounds, holding up a finger for each one as they say it, e.g. for "fl" they say "/f/, /l/" showing two fingers, and for "scr" they say "/s/,/c/,/r/," showing three fingers.

It is helpful for the students to think of examples of words with the blends in too.

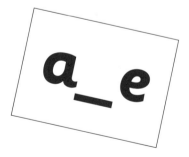

| sh | ch |
| th | ng |
| qu | or |

| ff | ll |
| ss | zz |
| ck | wh |

| a_e | i_e |
|---|---|
| o_e | u_e |
| ay | ea |

| igh | y |
| ow | ew |
| ou | oi |

| oy | ar |
| al | er |
| ir | ur |

nk

au

aw

| cl | bl |
|---|---|
| fl | gl |
| pl | sl |
| br | cr |

| dr | fr |
| gr | pr |
| tr | sc |
| sm | sn |

| sw | tw |
|----|----|
| sk | sp |
| nt | st |
| lb | ld |

| lf | lk |
| lm | lp |
| lt | ct |
| ft | pt |

| xt | mp |
| nd | spl |
| spr | str |
| scr | squ |

*Reproducible Section 4*

# Spelling and Tricky Word Sheets

Spelling List Sheets (pages 187-93)

Each week the students have a list of ten spelling words to take home and learn. The six Spelling List Sheets provide all the spelling lists ready to be reproduced, cut up, and pasted into the students' spelling homework books. To encourage parents to help their child, a parents' advice sheet has been provided. This can be copied, cut and pasted at the front of the spelling homework books. When the spelling tests have been graded, the results can be written into each book, to indicate to the parents how well their child has done.

Two tricky words are included in the weekly spelling list. However, it is useful to go over the tricky words separately as well. Two types of sheet are provided for extra practice.

Tricky Word Spelling List Sheet (page 194)

The Tricky Word Spelling Lists group together the twelve tricky words from each six weeks. They may be reproduced, cut up, and given out as an extra spelling homework, either in the holidays, or if there are any weeks to spare.

"Look, Copy, Cover, Write, Check" (pages 195-200)

The "Look, Copy, Cover, Write, Check" method is an effective way for the students to learn to spell tricky words. There is one sheet for each set of twelve tricky words. These can either be used in school, or given to the students to take home.

# Parents' Advice Sheet

*Dear Parent,*

Each week your child will be given ten spelling words. Please help him/her to learn them.

Most of the spelling words are regular. These can be spelled by listening for the sounds and writing the letter(s) for them.

The eighth and ninth words are irregular or "tricky," and have to be learned by heart. Once your child knows the names for all the letters in the alphabet, he/she can learn these harder words by saying the names of the letters in them, e.g. for the word "the," your child should say "tee aitch ee" several times each day, until the word is known.

# Spelling Lists 1-6

## 1. sh

1. am
2. get
3. clap
4. ship
5. fish
6. shut
7. wish
8. I
9. the
10. shampoo

## 2. ch

1. if
2. hot
3. blot
4. chips
5. lunch
6. chest
7. much
8. he
9. she
10. chicken

## 3. th

1. us
2. sad
3. flag
4. this
5. with
6. that
7. thank
8. me
9. we
10. thinking

## 4. ng

1. in
2. leg
3. glad
4. ring
5. sang
6. strong
7. lung
8. be
9. was
10. length

## 5. qu

1. on
2. but
3. plum
4. quick
5. quiz
6. queen
7. squid
8. to
9. do
10. squirrel

## 6. or

1. at
2. yes
3. slug
4. fork
5. storm
6. horse
7. forty
8. are
9. all
10. morning

# Spelling Lists 7-12

## 7. Days 1

1. it
2. dog
3. bran
4. Monday
5. Tuesday
6. Wednesday
7. Thursday
8. you
9. your
10. yesterday

## 8. Days 2

1. up
2. man
3. crab
4. Friday
5. Saturday
6. Sunday
7. today
8. come
9. some
10. weekend

## 9. ff

1. red
2. win
3. drum
4. off
5. cliff
6. stiff
7. cuff
8. said
9. here
10. puffin

## 10. ll

1. ox
2. run
3. from
4. will
5. bell
6. doll
7. skull
8. there
9. they
10. windmill

## 11. ss / zz

1. hop
2. fit
3. grin
4. buzz
5. cross
6. less
7. miss
8. go
9. no
10. classroom

## 12. ck

1. bed
2. wet
3. prod
4. duck
5. neck
6. clock
7. lick
8. so
9. my
10. backpack

# Spelling Lists 13-18

## 13. Colors

1. sad
2. let
3. trip
4. blue
5. orange
6. gray
7. black
8. one
9. by
10. color

## 14. a_e

1. ran
2. hat
3. scar
4. came
5. grape
6. name
7. cake
8. only
9. old
10. baseball

## 15. i_e

1. six
2. pad
3. smell
4. bike
5. time
6. smile
7. prize
8. like
9. have
10. bridesmaid

## 16. o_e

1. cod
2. lot
3. snap
4. bone
5. nose
6. home
7. globe
8. live
9. give
10. tadpole

## 17. u_e

1. bus
2. pot
3. swim
4. cube
5. tune
6. used
7. excuse
8. little
9. down
10. useless

## 18. wh

1. did
2. cut
3. twin
4. whale
5. wheel
6. white
7. whisper
8. what
9. when
10. whenever

# Spelling Lists 19-24

## 19. ay
1. an
2. cat
3. skin
4. say
5. away
6. play
7. today
8. why
9. where
10. playground

## 20. ea
1. met
2. web
3. spin
4. tea
5. heat
6. leaf
7. each
8. who
9. which
10. seashell

## 21. igh
1. lip
2. his
3. went
4. night
5. high
6. might
7. light
8. any
9. many
10. frightening

## 22. y
1. win
2. sit
3. stop
4. fry
5. dry
6. crying
7. sky
8. more
9. before
10. myself

## 23. ow
1. box
2. job
3. bulb
4. own
5. grow
6. elbow
7. yellow
8. other
9. were
10. snowman

## 24. ew
1. bud
2. sun
3. held
4. few
5. flew
6. grew
7. chew
8. because
9. want
10. newspaper

# Spelling Lists 25-30

## 25. ou

1. bat
2. pet
3. self
4. out
5. our
6. round
7. mouth
8. saw
9. put
10. outside

## 26. ow

1. big
2. fox
3. milk
4. how
5. owl
6. brown
7. town
8. could
9. should
10. flowerpot

## 27. oi

1. bug
2. had
3. film
4. oil
5. coin
6. noisy
7. spoiled
8. would
9. right
10. boiling

## 28. oy

1. jet
2. dig
3. help
4. boy
5. toy
6. enjoy
7. annoy
8. two
9. four
10. destroy

## 29. ar

1. got
2. bun
3. belt
4. arm
5. hard
6. scarf
7. cart
8. goes
9. does
10. barnyard

## 30. al

1. bad
2. vet
3. fact
4. all
5. talk
6. walk
7. small
8. made
9. their
10. beanstalk

# Spelling Lists 31-36

## 31. nk
1. fin
2. sob
3. left
4. sink
5. pink
6. drink
7. thank
8. once
9. upon
10. thinking

## 32. er
1. mud
2. jam
3. sent
4. herd
5. summer
6. river
7. number
8. always
9. also
10. woodpecker

## 33. ir
1. yet
2. hid
3. kept
4. skirt
5. girl
6. shirt
7. first
8. of
9. eight
10. birthday

## 34. ur
1. not
2. sum
3. next
4. turn
5. nurse
6. turkey
7. purple
8. love
9. cover
10. hamburger

## 35. au
1. map
2. fix
3. jump
4. fault
5. autumn
6. haunt
7. August
8. after
9. every
10. astronaut

## 36. aw
1. zip
2. men
3. pond
4. saw
5. claw
6. dawn
7. prawn
8. mother
9. father
10. strawberry

# Tricky Word Spelling Lists

1. I
2. the
3. he
4. she
5. me
6. we
7. be
8. was
9. to
10. do
11. are
12. all
13. you
14. your
15. come
16. some
17. said
18. here
19. there
20. they
21. go
22. no
23. so
24. my
25. one
26. by
27. only
28. old
29. like
30. have
31. live
32. give
33. little
34. down
35. what
36. when
37. why
38. where
39. who
40. which
41. any
42. many
43. more
44. before
45. other
46. were
47. because
48. want
49. saw
50. put
51. could
52. should
53. would
54. right
55. two
56. four
57. goes
58. does
59. made
60. their
61. once
62. upon
63. always
64. also
65. of
66. eight
67. love
68. cover
69. after
70. every
71. mother
72. father

| **Look** Say the letter names. | **Copy** Try writing the word. **Cover** | **Write** **Check** Is it right? | Have another try! |
|---|---|---|---|
| I | | | |
| the | | | |
| he | | | |
| she | | | |
| me | | | |
| we | | | |
| be | | | |
| was | | | |
| to | | | |
| do | | | |
| are | | | |
| all | | | |

| **Look** Say the letter names. | **Copy** Try writing the word. **Cover** | **Write** **Check** Is it right? | Have another try! |
|---|---|---|---|
| you | _____ | _____ | _____ |
| your | _____ | _____ | _____ |
| come | _____ | _____ | _____ |
| some | _____ | _____ | _____ |
| said | _____ | _____ | _____ |
| here | _____ | _____ | _____ |
| there | _____ | _____ | _____ |
| they | _____ | _____ | _____ |
| go | _____ | _____ | _____ |
| no | _____ | _____ | _____ |
| so | _____ | _____ | _____ |
| my | _____ | _____ | _____ |

| **Look** Say the letter names. | **Copy** Try writing the word. **Cover** | **Write** **Check** Is it right? | Have another try! |
|---|---|---|---|
| one | | | |
| by | | | |
| only | | | |
| old | | | |
| like | | | |
| have | | | |
| live | | | |
| give | | | |
| little | | | |
| down | | | |
| what | | | |
| when | | | |

| **Look** Say the letter names. | **Copy** Try writing the word. **Cover** | **Write** **Check** Is it right? | Have another try! |
|---|---|---|---|
| why | | | |
| where | | | |
| who | | | |
| which | | | |
| any | | | |
| many | | | |
| more | | | |
| before | | | |
| other | | | |
| were | | | |
| because | | | |
| want | | | |

| Look<br>Say the letter names. | Copy<br>Try writing the word.<br>Cover | Write<br>Check<br>Is it right? | Have another try! |
|---|---|---|---|
| saw | | | |
| put | | | |
| could | | | |
| should | | | |
| would | | | |
| right | | | |
| two | | | |
| four | | | |
| goes | | | |
| does | | | |
| made | | | |
| their | | | |

| Look<br>Say the letter names. | Copy<br>Try writing the word.<br>**Cover** | Write<br>**Check**<br>Is it right? | Have another try! |
|---|---|---|---|
| once | _____ | _____ | _____ |
| upon | _____ | _____ | _____ |
| always | _____ | _____ | _____ |
| also | _____ | _____ | _____ |
| of | _____ | _____ | _____ |
| eight | _____ | _____ | _____ |
| love | _____ | _____ | _____ |
| cover | _____ | _____ | _____ |
| after | _____ | _____ | _____ |
| every | _____ | _____ | _____ |
| mother | _____ | _____ | _____ |
| father | _____ | _____ | _____ |

*Reproducible Section 5*

# Alphabet Sheets

The students need to become thoroughly familiar with the order of the alphabet, as so many reference materials are organized in alphabetical order. There are two types of sheet provided for extra practice.

### Alphabet Letter Sets (pages 202-3)

These sheets may be reproduced and cut up to make sets of capital and lower-case alphabet letters. The sets can be used in a number of ways:

a. Give each student a letter, asking for its name and/or sound.

b. Give one student a complete set of capital or lower-case letters to arrange in alphabetical order (see Grammar 1, pages 28-9, and Grammar 4, pages 40-41).

c. Give one student a complete set of capital or lower-case letters to arrange into the four dictionary groups (see Grammar 7, pages 52-3). These are the groups into which the letters would fall, if a dictionary were divided into four approximately-equal parts:

1. Aa  Bb  Cc  Dd  Ee  (‹E› falls a quarter of the way through)
2. Ff  Gg  Hh  Ii  Jj  Kk  Ll  Mm  (‹M› falls halfway through)
3. Nn  Oo  Pp  Qq  Rr  Ss  (‹S› falls three quarters of the way through)
4. Tt  Uu  Vv  Ww  Xx  Yy  Zz

d. Sit the students in a circle and give each of them a letter. Call out a regular word. Those students, whose letters are in the word, use them to spell the word in the middle of the circle. This is also a good way of practicing the tricky words.

### Alphabet Writing Card (page 204)

This sheet may be reproduced, pasted onto card and laminated. A piece of tracing paper may be clipped to the card, for one of the students to practice writing out the alphabet (See Grammar 4, pages 40-41).

# Alphabet Letter Set – Lower-case

| a | b | c | d |
|---|---|---|---|
| e | f | g | h |
| i | j | k | l |
| m | n | o | p |
| q | r | s | t |
| u | v | w | x |
| y | z |  |  |

# Alphabet Letter Set – Capitals

| A | B | C | D |
| E | F | G | H |
| I | J | K | L |
| M | N | O | P |
| Q | R | S | T |
| U | V | W | X |
| Y | Z | | |

Aa Bb Cc Dd Ee Ff Gg Hh Ii Jj Kk Ll Mm Nn Oo Pp Qq Rr Ss Tt Uu Vv Ww Xx Yy Zz

*Reproducible Section 6*

# "Sentence Pasting" Sheets

The "Sentence Pasting" Sheets can be used with Grammar sheet 2 (page 33), so that the students do not all have the same sentence to unscramble. Alternatively the sheets can be used as an extension activity. Each pair of sentence pasting exercises is harder than the one before.

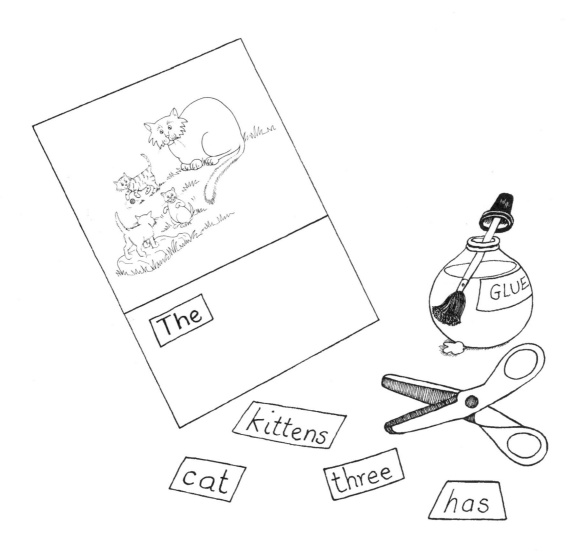

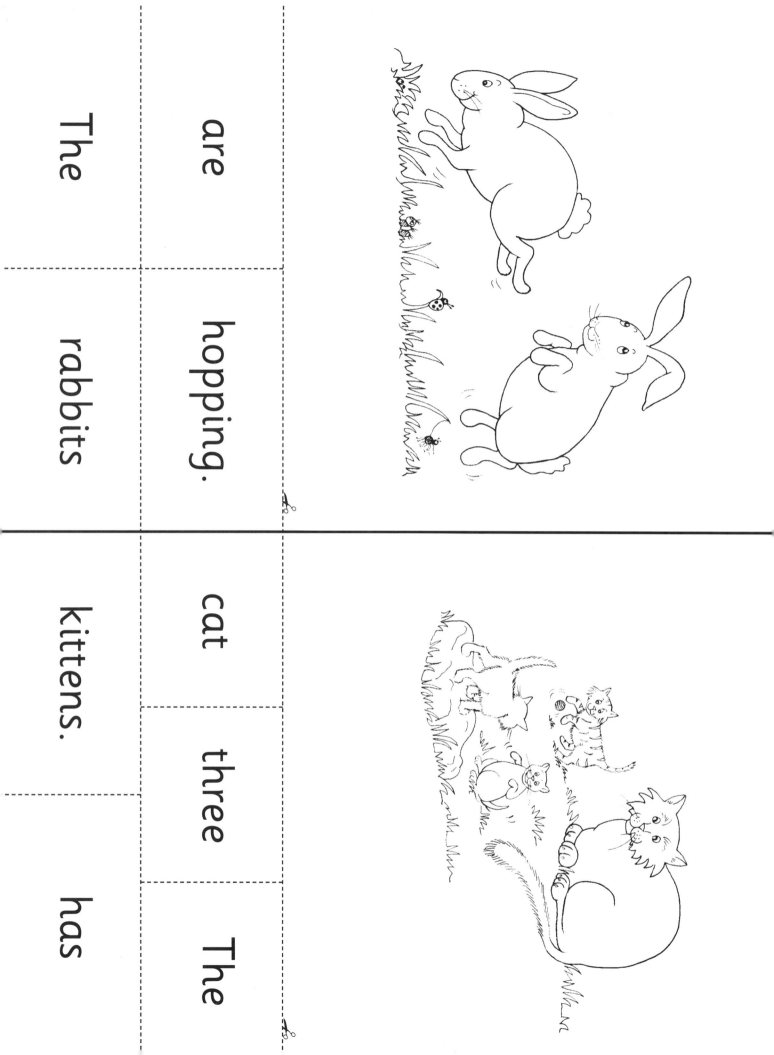

The rabbits are hopping.

The cat has three kittens.

| nest. | The | chicks | run | to | the |
|---|---|---|---|---|---|
| very | dirty. | tractor | red | is | The |

| swings | There | the |
| --- | --- | --- |
| slide | in | and |
| are | a | park. |

| she | the |
| --- | --- |
| buzzed | collected |
| from | flowers. |
| Bee | as |
|  | pollen |

*Reproducible Section 7*

# "Pull-Out Plurals" Sheet

This sheet can be used as a fun extension activity. The students choose a noun and draw a picture for it, in the top frame. Then they draw two or more pictures of the same thing, in the second frame. They cut out both pieces, cut the slits as indicated, and fit the two pieces together. They have to cut very carefully to make the "pull-out plural" work. This exercise offers the students a multisensory way of understanding the concept of plurals (see Grammar 9, pages 60-61).

# Pull-Out Plurals

Draw something in the top frame.
Draw more than one of the same thing in the lower frame.
Cut out the 2 pieces. Cut the slits in the rectangle. Put in your pull-out plural.

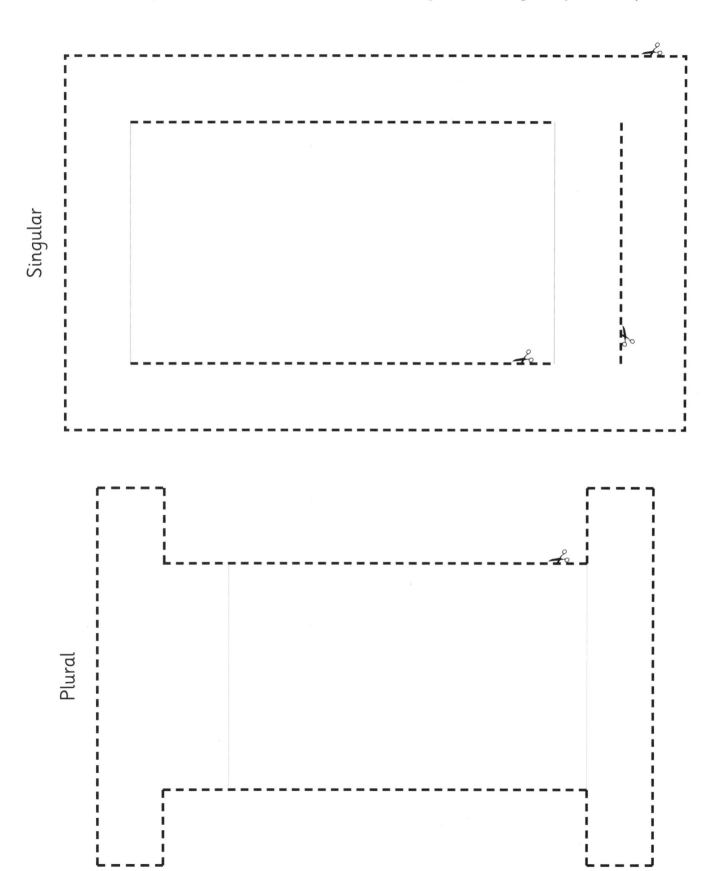

*Reproducible Section 8*

# "Verb Bees" Sheet

The students can use this big bee shape to make their own "busy verb bees."

The outlined bee shape may be reproduced, or used to make a card template. The students each choose a verb, and then add wings, legs, etc. to show their bee performing it. They can look at the bees on Grammar sheet 14 (page 81), or the verbs page in the *Jolly Grammar Big Book 1*, for ideas. The big bees can then be used to make a verb display.

*Reproducible Section 9*

# "Adjective Snake" Sheets

The outlined snake sections may be reproduced for the students to make "adjective snakes," either in groups or individually. Any number of middle (body) sections can be used between the snake's head and tail.

The students colour each body section of the snake in a different way, and write or stick on an adjective (e.g. "red," "sad," "scaly," "spotty") to describe it. (See the snakes on Grammar sheet 21, page 109, or the adjectives sheet in the *Jolly Grammar Big Book 1,* for ideas.) The sections may be stuck together to make an "adjective snake" for display.

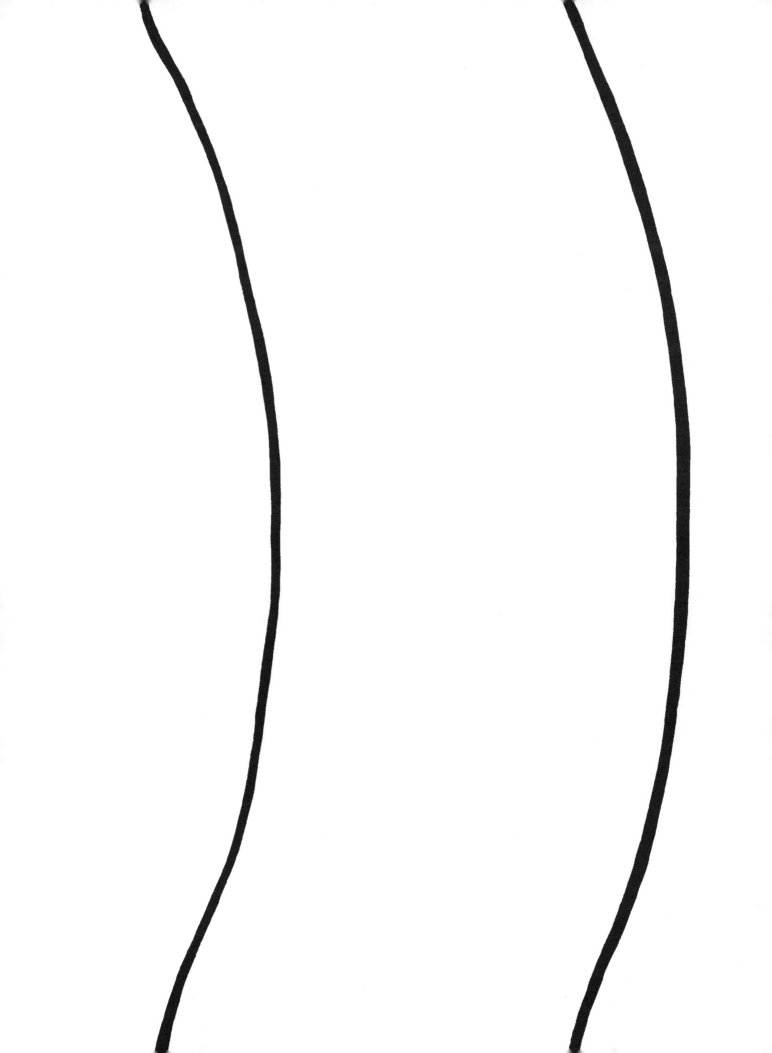

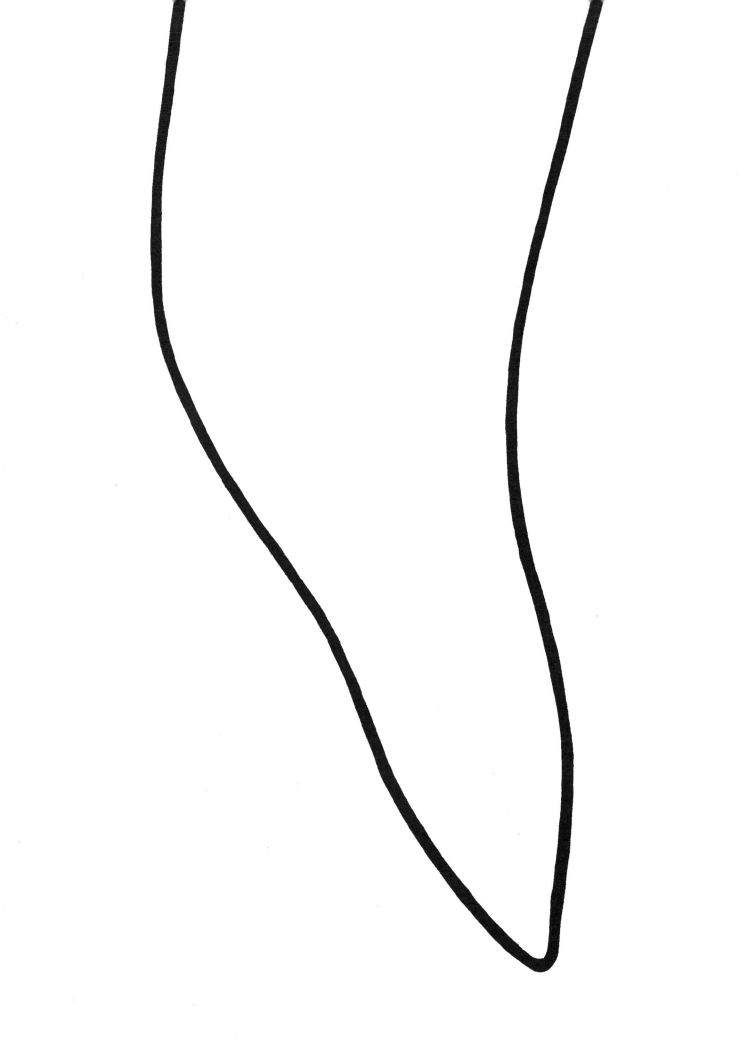

*Reproducible Section 10*

# "Compound Birds" Sheet

The "compound birds" sheet may be reproduced and cut up to make sets of compound word puzzles. Use the copy machine to enlarge them if preferred. Then write the first part of a compound word on the body, and the second part on the tail, of each bird. (See Grammar sheet 24, page 121, or the Compound Birds sheet in the *Jolly Grammar Big Book 1,* for ideas.) Muddle up the pieces and see if the students can match the birds to their tails, by reading the words.

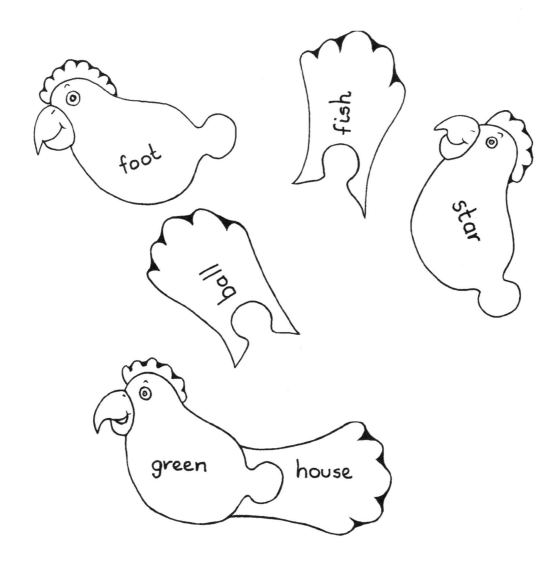

# Compound Birds